EVERYMAN,
I WILL GO WITH THEE
AND BE THY GUIDE,
IN THY MOST NEED
TO GO BY THY SIDE

EVERYMAN'S LIBRARY
POCKET POETS

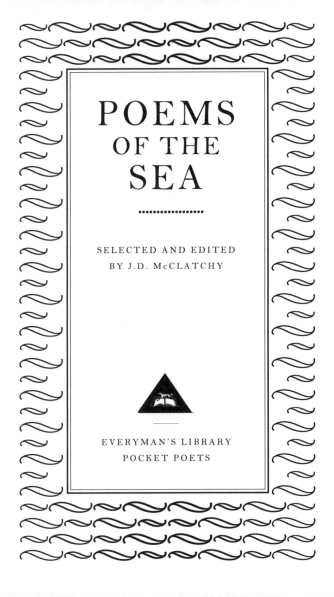

POEMS
OF THE
SEA

....

SELECTED AND EDITED
BY J.D. McCLATCHY

EVERYMAN'S LIBRARY
POCKET POETS

This selection by J.D. McClatchy first published in
Everyman's Library, 2001
© Everyman Publishers plc, 2001

A list of acknowledgments to copyright owners appears at the back of
this volume.

ISBN 1-84159-746-5

A CIP catalogue record for this book is available from the British Library

Published by Everyman Publishers plc,
Gloucester Mansions, 140A Shaftesbury Avenue, London WC2H 8HD

Distributed by Random House (UK) Ltd.,
20 Vauxhall Bridge Road, London SW1V 2SA

Typography by Peter B. Willberg
Typeset in the UK by AccComputing, North Barrow, Somerset
Printed and bound in Germany by GGP Media, Pössneck

CONTENTS

STORM AND CALM

BALLADS

SONGS AND CHANTEYS

READING THE WAVES

FOREWORD

At least since Darwin's day, we have known that all of us originally emerged from the sea. That fact may in part account for our abiding fascination with it, our longing to return there, whether to sail the main or merely contemplate its restless enormity. Surely it's not accidental that we refer to "bodies of water", when we think how, from the very beginning, men have explored its secluded coves and furthest reaches. Our continents have been carried, grain by grain, in its deeps. The earth's wind and rain rise from it. Like our bodies, the globe itself is mostly water, the ocean river of time circling, sweeping us towards our beginning and our end.

Until the twentieth century, when we could fly over it, the sea dominated the strategies of human movement and imagination. The dangers, the legends, the lore, the life of the sea preoccupied our singers as well. The tide's own rise and fall gave a rhythm to their accounts. Anonymous ballads and riddles, prayers and chanteys attest to the ancient effort to placate the sea's power. Nothing more mysterious – so huge and unpredictable, placid and ferocious, nurturing and destructive – has ever appeared before our eyes, and it is only natural that our poets, from the author of Genesis on, have been drawn to describe its vast surround. Homer's intrepid heroes brave its storms and monsters. Shakespeare gazes down the full fathoms five. Milton thunders on the torrent rapture and watery ooze. In many ways, the ocean has been like a mighty mirror, reflecting the anxieties and astonishment of the poets themselves. Like mariners, they ply the surface and speculate on the depths.

Poems about the sea would be cargo for a fleet. Those in this anthology's little ketch have been chosen to represent the extraordinary variety of voices. From shipboard work-songs like "Blow the Man Down" to Longfellow's stirring ballads, from Emily Dickinson's exultant fancies to Hart Crane's ecstatic dirges, from "Casabianca" ("The boy stood on the burning deck") to "The Rhyme of the Ancient Mariner" ("Water, water everywhere/Nor any drop to drink"), from Tennyson's mermaid and Poe's Annabel Lee to Melville's Billy and T. S. Eliot's Marina – here are enthralling poems, both familiar and new, salty and sublime, that remind us why in each reader's heart there echoes a single refrain: "I must go down to the sea again". As you stand on the shores of this book, you will see beyond its horizon the ocean's expanse of pleasures and perils. And here are the poets, putting into words an immensity that only the imagination can contain.

J. D. McCLATCHY

SEA-FEVER

"EXULTATION IS THE GOING"

Exultation is the going
Of an inland soul to sea –
Past the houses, past the headlands,
Into deep Eternity!

Bred as we, among the mountains,
Can the sailor understand
The divine intoxication
Of the first league out from land?

SEA LONGING

A thousand miles beyond this sun-steeped wall
  Somewhere the waves creep cool along the sand,
  The ebbing tide forsakes the listless land
With the old murmur, long and musical;
The windy waves mount up and curve and fall,
  And round the rocks the foam blows up like snow –
  Tho' I am inland far, I hear and know,
For I was born the sea's eternal thrall.
I would that I were there and over me
  The cold insistence of the tide would roll,
  Quenching this burning thing men call the soul, –
Then with the ebbing I should drift and be
  Less than the smallest shell along the shoal,
Less than the seagulls calling to the sea.

THE RETURN

I will go back to the great sweet mother,
   Mother and lover of men, the sea.
I will go down to her, I and none other,
   Close with her, kiss her and mix her with me;
Cling to her, strive with her, hold her fast;
O fair white mother, in days long past
Born without sister, born without brother,
   Set free my soul as thy soul is free.

O fair green-girdled mother of mine,
   Sea, that art clothed with the sun and the rain,
Thy sweet hard kisses are strong like wine,
   Thy large embraces are keen like pain.
Save me and hide me with all thy waves,
Find me one grave of thy thousand graves,
Those pure cold populous graves of thine,
   Wrought without hand in a world without stain.

I shall sleep, and move with the moving ships,
   Change as the winds change, veer in the tide;
My lips will feast on the foam of thy lips,
   I shall rise with thy rising, with thee subside;
Sleep, and now know if she be, if she were,
Filled full with life to the eyes and hair,
As a rose is fulfilled to the roseleaf tips
   With splendid summer and perfume and pride.

This woven raiment of nights and days,
    Were it once cast off and unwound from me,
Naked and glad would I walk in thy ways,
    Alive and aware of thy ways and thee;
Clear of the whole world, hidden at home,
Clothed with the green and crowned with the foam,
A pulse of the life of thy straits and bays,
    A vein in the heart of the streams of the sea.

MANA OF THE SEA

Do you see the sea, breaking itself to bits against
    the islands
yet remaining unbroken, the level great sea?

Have I caught from it
the tide in my arms
that runs down to the shallows of my wrists,
    and breaks
abroad in my hands, like waves among the rocks
    of substance?

Do the rollers of the sea
roll down my thighs
and over the submerged islets of my knees
with power, sea-power
sea-power
to break against the ground
in the flat, recurrent breakers of my two feet?

And is my body ocean, ocean
whose power runs to the shores along my arms
and breaks in the foamy hands, whose power rolls out
to the white-treading waves of two salt feet?

I am the sea, I am the sea!

SEAFARER

The sea will wash in
but the rocks – jagged ribs
riding the cloth of foam
or a knob or pinnacles
    with gannets –
are the stubborn man.

He invites the storm, he
lives by it! instinct
with fears that are not fears
but prickles of ecstasy,
a secret liquor, a fire
that inflames his blood to
coldness so that the rocks
seem rather to leap
at the sea than the sea
to envelop them. They strain
forward to grasp ships
or even the sky itself that
bends down to be torn
upon them. To which he says,
It is I! I who am the rocks!
Without me nothing laughs.

EXILED

Searching my heart for its true sorrow,
　　This is the thing I find to be:
That I am weary of words and people,
　　Sick of the city, wanting the sea;

Wanting the sticky, salty sweetness
　　Of the strong wind and shattered spray;
Wanting the loud sound and the soft sound
　　Of the big surf that breaks all day.

Always before about my dooryard,
　　Marking the reach of the winter sea,
Rooted in sand and dragging drift-wood,
　　Straggled the purple wild sweet-pea;

Always I climbed the wave at morning,
　　Shook the sand from my shoes at night,
That now am caught beneath great buildings,
　　Stricken with noise, confused with light.

If I could hear the green piles groaning
　　Under the windy wooden piers,
See once again the bobbing barrels,
　　And the black sticks that fence the weirs,

If I could see the weedy mussels
    Crusting the wrecked and rotting hulls,
Hear once again the hungry crying
    Overhead, of the wheeling gulls,

Feel once again the shanty straining
    Under the turning of the tide,
Fear once again the rising freshet,
    Dread the bell in the fog outside,

I should be happy, – that was happy
    All day long on the coast of Maine!
I have a need to hold and handle
    Shells and anchors and ships again!

I should be happy, that am happy
    Never at all since I came here.
I am too long away from water.
    I have a need of water near.

SEA-FEVER

I must go down to the seas again, to the lonely sea
    and the sky,
And all I ask is a tall ship and a star to steer her by,
And the wheel's kick and the wind's song,
    and the white sail's shaking,
And a grey mist on the sea's face and a grey dawn
    breaking.

I must go down to the seas again, for the call of
    the running tide
Is a wild call and a clear call that may not be denied;
And all I ask is a windy day with the white clouds
    flying,
And the flung spray and the blown spume, and the
    sea-gulls crying.

I must go down to the seas again, to the vagrant
    gypsy life,
To the gull's way and the whale's way where the
    wind's like a whetted knife;
And all I ask is a merry yarn from a laughing
    fellow-rover,
And quiet sleep and a sweet dream when the long
    trick's over.

JOHN MASEFIELD

THE CALL OF
THE DEEP

From PARADISE LOST, BOOK VII

                       Over all the face of earth
Main ocean flow'd, not idle, but with warm
Prolific humor soft'ning all her globe
Fermented the great mother to conceive,
Satiate with genial moisture, when God said,
Be gather'd now, ye waters under heaven,
Into one place, and let dry land appear.
Immediately the mountains huge appear
Emergent, and their broad bare backs upheave
Into the clouds, their tops ascend the sky.
So high as heav'd the tumid hills, so low
Down sunk a hollow bottom broad and deep,
Capacious bed of waters: thither they
Hasted with glad precipitance, uproll'd
As drops on dust conglobing from the dry:
Part rise in crystal wall, or ridge direct,
For haste; such flight the great command imprest
On the swift floods: as armies at the call
Of trumpet, for of armies thou hast heard,
Troop to their standard, so the wat'ry throng,
Wave rolling after wave, where way they found;
If steep, with torrent rapture, if through plain,
Soft-ebbing; nor withstood them rock or hill,
But they, or under ground, or circuit wide
With serpent error wand'ring, found their way,

And on the washy ooze deep channels wore,
Easy, ere God had bid the ground be dry,
All but within those banks, where rivers now
Stream, and perpetual draw their humid train.
The dry land Earth, and the great receptacle
Of congregated waters He call'd Seas.

From CHILDE HAROLD'S PILGRIMAGE

Roll on, thou deep and dark blue Ocean – roll!
Ten thousand fleets sweep over thee in vain;
Man marks the earth with ruin – his control
Stops with the shore; – upon the watery plain
The wrecks are all thy deed, nor doth remain
A shadow of man's ravage, save his own,
When, for a moment, like a drop of rain,
He winks into thy depths with bubbling groan,
Without a grave, unknell'd, uncoffin'd, and unknown.

His steps are not upon thy paths, – thy fields
Are not a spoil for him, – thou dost arise
And shake him from thee; the vile strength he wields
For earth's destruction thou dost all despise,
Spurning him from thy bosom to the skies,
And send'st him, shivering in thy playful spray,
And howling, to his gods, where haply lies
His petty hope in some near port or bay,
And dashest him again to earth: – there let him lay.

The armaments which thunderstrike the walls
Of rock-built cities, bidding nations quake,
And monarchs tremble in their capitals,
The oak leviathans, whose huge ribs make
Their clay creator the vain title take

Of lord of thee, and arbiter of war;
　These are thy toys, and, as the snowy flake,
　They melt into thy yeast of waves, which mar
Alike the Armada's pride, or spoils of Trafalgar.

　Thy shores are empires, changed in all save thee –
　Assyria, Greece, Rome, Carthage, what are they?
　Thy waters washed them power while they were free,
　And many a tyrant since: their shores obey
　The stranger, slave, or savage; their decay
　Has dried up realms to deserts: not so thou;
　Unchangeable save to thy wild waves' play –
　Time writes no wrinkles on thine azure brow –
Such as creation's dawn beheld, thou rollest now.

　Thou glorious mirror, where the Almighty's form
　Glasses itself in tempests; in all time,
　Calm, or convulsed – in breeze, or gale, or storm,
　Icing the pole, or in the torrid clime
　Dark-heaving; boundless, endless, and sublime –
　The image of Eternity – the throne
　Of the Invisible; even from out thy slime
　The monsters of the deep are made; each zone
Obeys thee; thou goest forth, dread, fathomless, alone.

And I have loved thee, Ocean! and my joy
Of youthful sports was on thy breast to be
Borne like thy bubbles, onward: from a boy
I wanton'd with thy breakers – they to me
Were a delight; and if the freshening sea
Made them a terror – 'twas a pleasing fear,
For I was as it were a child of thee,
And trusted to thy billows far and near,
And laid my hand upon thy mane – as I do here.

From QUEEN MAB

– Those trackless depths, where many a weary sail
Has seen, above the illimitable plain,
Morning and night, and night on morning rise;
Whilst still no land to greet the wanderer spread
Its shadowy mountains on the sun-bright sea,
Where the loud roaring of the tempest-waves
So long have mingled with the gusty wind
In melancholy loneliness, and swept
The desert of those ocean solitudes;
But, vocal to the sea-bird's harrowing shriek,
The bellowing monster and the rushing storm,
Now to the sweet and many-mingling sounds
Of kindliest human impulses respond.

ON THE SEA

It keeps eternal whisperings around
   Desolate shores, and with its mighty swell
   Gluts twice ten thousand caverns, till the spell
Of Hecate leaves them their old shadowy sound.
Often 'tis in such gentle temper found,
   That scarcely will the very smallest shell
   Be moved for days from whence it sometime fell,
When last the winds of heaven were unbound.
Oh ye! who have your eye-balls vexed and tired,
   Feast them upon the wideness of the Sea;
     Oh ye! whose ears are dinned with uproar rude,
   Or fed too much with cloying melody, –
     Sit ye near some old cavern's mouth, and brood
Until ye start, as if the sea-nymphs quired!

THE SEA LIMITS

Consider the sea's listless chime:
    Time's self it is, made audible, –
    The murmur of the earth's own shell.
Secret continuance sublime
    Is the sea's end: our sight may pass
    No furlong further. Since time was,
This sound has told the lapse of time.

No quiet, which is death's, – it hath
    The mournfulness of ancient life,
    Enduring always at dull strife.
As the world's heart of rest and wrath,
    Its painful pulse is in the sands.
    Lost utterly, the whole sky stands,
Grey and not known, along its path.

Listen, alone beside the sea,
    Listen alone among the woods;
    Those voices of twin solitudes
Shall have one sound alike to thee:
    Hark where the murmurs of thronged men
    Surge and sink back and surge again, –
Still the one voice of wave and tree.

Gather a shell from the strewn beach
   And listen at its lips: they sigh
   The same desire and mystery,
The echo of the whole sea's speech.
   And all mankind is thus at heart
   Not anything but what thou art:
And Earth, Sea, Man, are all in each.

BY THE SEA

Why does the sea moan evermore?
  Shut out from heaven it makes its moan,
It frets against the boundary shore;
  All earth's full rivers cannot fill
  The sea, that drinking thirsteth still.

Sheer miracles of loveliness
  Lie hid in its unlooked-on bed:
Anemones, salt, passionless,
  Blow flower-like; just enough alive
  To blow and multiply and thrive.

Shells quaint with curve, or spot, or spike,
  Encrusted live things argus-eyed,
All fair alike, yet all unlike,
  Are born without a pang, and die
  Without a pang, and so pass by.

MAN AND SEA

Man – a free man – always loves the sea
and in its endlessly unrolling surge
will contemplate his soul as in a glass
where gulfs as bitter gape within his mind.

Into this image of himself he dives,
his arms and eyes wide open and his heart
sometimes diverted from its own dead march
by the tides of that untamable complaint.

How grim their combat, and yet how discreet
– who has sounded to its depths the human heart?
and who has plucked its riches from the sea? –
so jealously they guard their secrets, both!

Countless the ages past and still to come
in which they wage their unrelenting war
for sheer delight in carnage and in death,
implacable brothers and eternal foes!

CHARLES BAUDELAIRE   37
TRANSLATED BY RICHARD HOWARD

THE SEA

From the zenith piercing the azure the sun glitters
In the sea's orbicular and blue mirror.
The golden arrows hurling from the fiery sky's height
Are heavily engulfed in the calm flat main.

And the odorous swell of the open sea dilates
Sinuously lengthens and then rises slightly
Like a sacred serpent under the fixed gaze of a God.
Day sinks. The surge is steeped in scarlet.

Sunk in the ocean of translucent blazonries
The sun, as a dying bird plunges, has set,
And evening's gold is lost in the Eternal tomb.

A wave scarcely rises and then falls
Whilst the beauty in the gloomy crepe spreads –
Night the mysterious with her numberless eyes.

THE SOUND OF THE SEA

The sea awoke at midnight from its sleep,
 And round the pebbly beaches far and wide
 I heard the first wave of the rising tide
 Rush onward with uninterrupted sweep;
A voice out of the silence of the deep,
 A sound mysteriously multiplied
 As of a cataract from the mountain's side,
 Or roar of winds upon a wooded steep.
So comes to us at times, from the unknown
 And inaccessible solitudes of being,
 The rushing of the sea-tides of the soul;
And inspirations, that we deem our own,
 Are some divine foreshadowing and foreseeing
 Of things beyond our reason or control.

HENRY WADSWORTH LONGFELLOW

VOYAGES, II

– And yet this great wink of eternity,
Of rimless floods, unfettered leewardings,
Samite sheeted and processioned where
Her undinal vast belly moonward bends,
Laughing the wrapt inflections of our love;

Take this Sea, whose diapason knells
On scrolls of silver snowy sentences,
The sceptred terror of whose sessions rends
As her demeanors motion well or ill,
All but the pieties of lovers' hands.

And onward, as bells off San Salvador
Salute the crocus lustres of the stars,
In these poinsettia meadows of her tides, –
Adagios of islands, O my Prodigal,
Complete the dark confessions her veins spell.

Mark how her turning shoulders wind the hours,
And hasten while her penniless rich palms
Pass superscription of bent foam and wave, –
Hasten, while they are true, – sleep, death, desire,
Close round one instant in one floating flower.

Bind us in time, O Seasons clear, and awe.
O minstrel galleons of Carib fire,
Bequeath us to no earthly shore until
Is answered in the vortex of our grave
The seal's wide spindrift gaze toward paradise.

FULL FATHOM FIVE

Old man, you surface seldom.
Then you come in with the tide's coming
When seas wash cold, foam-

Capped: white hair, white beard, far-flung,
A dragnet, rising, falling, as waves
Crest and trough. Miles long

Extend the radial sheaves
Of your spread hair, in which wrinkling skeins
Knotted, caught, survives

The old myth of origins
Unimaginable. You float near
As keeled ice-mountains

Of the north, to be steered clear
Of, not fathomed. All obscurity
Starts with a danger:

Your dangers are many. I
Cannot look much but your form suffers
Some strange injury

And seems to die: so vapors
Ravel to clearness on the dawn sea.
The muddy rumors

Of your burial move me
To half-believe: your reappearance
Proves rumors shallow,

For the archaic trenched lines
Of your grained face shed time in runnels:
Ages beat like rains

On the unbeaten channels
Of the ocean. Such sage humor and
Durance are whirlpools

To make away with the ground –
Work of the earth and the sky's ridgepole.
Waist down, you may wind

One labyrinthine tangle
To root deep among knuckles, shinbones,
Skulls. Inscrutable,

Below shoulders not once
Seen by any man who kept his head,
You defy questions;

You defy other godhood.
I walk dry on your kingdom's border
Exiled to no good.

Your shelled bed I remember.
Father, this thick air is murderous.
I would breathe water.

STORM AND CALM

From THE STORM

The south and west winds joined, and, as they blew,
Waves like a rolling trench before them threw.
Sooner than you read this line, did the gale,
Like shot, not feared till felt, our sails assail;
And what at first was called a gust, the same
Hath now a storm's, anon a tempest's name.
Jonas, I pity thee, and curse those men,
Who, when the storm raged most, did wake thee then;
Sleep is pain's easiest salve, and doth fulfill
All offices of death, except to kill.
But when I waked, I saw that I saw not;
Ay, and the sun, which should teach me, had forgot
East, west, day, night, and I could only say,
If the world had lasted, now it had been day.
Thousands our noises were, yet we 'mongst all
Could none by his right name, but thunder call.
Lightning was all our light, and it rained more
Than if the sun had drunk the sea before.
Some coffin'd in their cabins lie, equally
Grieved that they are not dead, and yet must die;
And as sin-burdened souls from graves will creep
At the last day, some forth their cabins peep,
And tremblingly ask, "What news?" and do hear so,
Like jealous husbands, what they would not know.
Some, sitting on the hatches, would seem there

With hideous gazing to fear away fear.
Then note they the ship's sicknesses, the mast
Shaked with this ague, and the hold and waist
With a salt dropsy clogged, and all our tacklings
Snapping, like too-high-stretched treble strings,
And from our tattered sails rags drop down so,
As from one hanged in chains a year ago.
Even our ordnance placed for our defence,
Strives to break loose, and 'scape away from thence.
Pumping hath tired our men, and what's the gain?
Seas into seas thrown, we suck in again;
Hearing hath deaf'd our sailors, and if they
Knew how to hear, there's none knows what to say.
Compared to these storms death is but a qualm,
Hell somewhat lightsome, the Bermudas calm.
Darkness, light's elder brother, his birthright
Claims o'er this world, and to heaven hath chased light.
All things are one, and that one none can be,
Since all forms uniform deformity
Doth cover; so that we, except God say
Another Fiat, shall have no more day:
So violent, yet long these furies be.

A VISION OF THE SEA

'Tis the terror of tempest. The rags of the sail
Are flickering in ribbons within the fierce gale:
From the stark night of vapours the dim rain is driven,
And when lightning is loosed, like a deluge from
      Heaven,
She sees the black trunks of the waterspouts spin
And bend, as if Heaven was running in,
Which they seemed to sustain with their terrible mass
As if ocean had sunk from beneath them: they pass
To their graves in the deep with an earthquake of sound,
And the waves and the thunders, made silent around,
Leave the wind to its echo. The vessel, now tossed
Through the low-trailing rack of the tempest, is lost
In the skirts of the thunder-cloud: now down the sweep
Of the wind-cloven wave to the chasm of the deep
It sinks, and the walls of the watery vale
Whose depths of dread calm are unmoved by the gale,
Dim mirrors of ruin, hang gleaming about;
While the surf, like a chaos of stars, like a rout
Of death-flames, like whirlpools of fire-flowing iron,
With splendour and terror the black ship environ,
Or like sulphur-flakes hurled from a mine of pale fire
In fountains spout o'er it. In many a spire
The pyramid-billows with white points of brine
In the cope of the lightning inconstantly shine,

As piercing the sky from the floor of the sea,
The great ship seems splitting! it cracks as a tree,
While an earthquake is splintering its root, ere the blast
Of the whirlwind that stripped it of branches has passed.
The intense thunder-balls which are raining
        from Heaven
Have shattered its mast, and it stands black and riven.
The chinks suck destruction. The heavy dead hulk
On the living sea rolls an inanimate bulk,
Like a corpse on the clay which is hungering to fold
Its corruption around it. Meanwhile, from the hold,
One deck is burst up by the waters below,
And it splits like the ice when the thaw-breezes blow
O'er the lakes of the desert! Who sit on the other?
Is that all the crew that like burying each other,
Like the dead in a breach, round the foremast? Are those
Twin tigers, who burst, when the waters arose,
In the agony of terror, their chains in the hold;
(What now makes them tame, is what then made
        them bold;)
Who crouch side by side, and have driven, like a crank,
The deep grip of their claws through the vibrating
        plank: –
Are these all? Nine weeks the tall vessel had lain
On the windless expanse of the watery plain,
Where the death-darting sun cast no shadow at noon,
And there seemed to be fire in the beams of the moon,

Till a lead-coloured fog gathered up from the deep,
Whose breath was quick pestilence; then, the cold sleep
Crept, like blight through the ears of a thick field
        of corn,
O'er the populous vessel. And even and morn,
With their hammocks for coffins, the seamen aghast
Like dead men the dead limbs of their comrades cast
Down the deep, which closed on them above and around,
And the sharks and the dogfish their grave-clothes
        unbound,
And were glutted like Jews with this manna rained down
From God on their wilderness. One after one
The mariners died; on the eve of this day,
When the tempest was gathering in cloudy array,
But seven remained. Six the thunder has smitten,
And they lie black as mummies on which Time
        has written
His scorn of the embalmer; the seventh, from the deck
An oak-splinter pierced through his breast and his back,
And hung out to the tempest, a wreck on the wreck.
No more? At the helm sits a woman more fair
Than Heaven, when, unbinding its star-braided hair,
It sinks with the sun on the earth and the sea.
She clasps a bright child on her upgathered knee;
It laughs at the lightning, it mocks the mixed thunder
Of the air and the sea, with desire and with wonder
It is beckoning the tigers to rise and come near,

It would play with those eyes where the radiance of fear
Is outshining the meteors; its bosom beats high,
The heart-fire of pleasure has kindled its eye,
While its mother's is lustreless. "Smile not, my child,
But sleep deeply and sweetly, and so be beguiled
Of the pang that awaits us, whatever that be,
So dreadful since thou must divide it with me!
Dream, sleep! This pale bosom, thy cradle and bed,
Will it rock thee not, infant? 'Tis beating with dread!
Alas! what is life, what is death, what are we,
That when the ship sinks we no longer may be?
What! to see thee no more, and to feel thee no more?
Not to be after life what we have been before?
Not to touch those sweet hands? Not to look on
        those eyes,
Those lips, and that hair, – all that smiling disguise
Thou yet wearest, sweet Spirit, which I, day by day,
Have so long called my child, but which now fades away
Like a rainbow, and I the fallen shower?" – Lo! the ship
Is settling, it topples, the leeward ports dip;
The tigers leap up when they feel the slow brine
Crawling inch by inch on them; hair, ears, limbs,
        and eyne,
Stand rigid with horror; a loud, long, hoarse cry
Bursts at once from their vitals tremendously,
And 'tis borne down the mountainous vale of the wave,
Rebounding, like thunder, from crag to cave,

Mixed with the clash of the lashing rain,
Hurried on by the might of the hurricane:
The hurricane came from the west, and passed on
By the path of the gate of the eastern sun,
Transversely dividing the stream of the storm;
As an arrowy serpent, pursuing the form
Of an elephant, bursts through the brakes of the waste.
Black as a cormorant, the screaming blast,
Between Ocean and Heaven, like an ocean, passed,
Till it came to the clouds on the verge of the world
Which, based on the sea and to Heaven upcurled,
Like columns and walls did surround and sustain
The dome of the tempest; it rent them in twain,
As a flood rends its barriers of mountainous crag:
And the dense clouds in many a ruin and rag,
Like the stones of a temple ere earthquake has passed,
Like the dust of its fall, on the whirlwind are cast;
They are scattered like foam on the torrent; and where
The wind has burst out through the chasm, from the air
Of clear morning the beams of the sunrise flow in,
Unimpeded, keen, golden, and crystalline,
Banded armies of light and of air: at one gate
They encounter, but interpenetrate.
And that breach in the tempest is widening away,
And the caverns of clouds are torn up by the day,
And the fierce winds are sinking with weary wings,
Lulled by the motion and murmurings

And the long grassy heave of the rocking sea;
And overhead glorious, but dreadful to see,
The wrecks of the tempest, like vapours of gold,
Are consuming at sunrise. The heaped waves behold
The deep calm of blue Heaven dilating above,
And, like passions made still by the presence of Love,
Beneath the clear surface reflecting it slide
Tremulous with soft influence; extending its tide
From the Andes to Atlas, round mountain and isle,
Round sea-birds and wrecks, paved with Heaven's
    azure smile,
The wide world of waters is vibrating. Where
Is the ship? On the verge of the wave where it lay
One tiger is mingled in ghastly affray
With a sea-snake. The foam and the smoke of the battle
Stain the clear air with sunbows; the jar, and the rattle
Of solid bones crushed by the infinite stress
Of the snake's adamantine voluminousness;
And the hum of the hot blood that spouts and rains
Where the grip of the tiger has wounded the veins
Swollen with rage, strength, and effort; the whirl
    and the splash
As of some hideous engine whose brazen teeth smash
The thin winds and soft waves into thunder; the streams
And hissings crawl fast o'er the smooth ocean-streams,
Each sound like a centipede. Near this commotion,
A blue shark is hanging within the blue ocean,

The fin-winged tomb of the victor. The other
Is winning his way from the fate of his brother
To his own with the speed of despair. Lo! a boat
Advances; twelve rowers with the impulse of thought
Urge on the keen keel, – the brine foams. At the stern
Three marksmen stand levelling. Hot bullets burn
In the breast of the tiger, which yet bears him on
To his refuge and ruin. One fragment alone, –
'Tis dwindling and sinking, 'tis now almost gone,
Of the wreck of the vessel peers out of the sea,
With her left hand she grasps it impetuously,
With her right she sustains her fair infant. Death, Fear,
Love, Beauty are mixed in the atmosphere,
Which trembles and burns with the fervour of dread
Around her wild eyes, her bright hand, and her head,
Like a meteor of light o'er the waters! her child
Is yet smiling, and playing, and murmuring; so smiled
The false deep ere the storm. Like a sister and brother
The child and the ocean still smile on each other,
Whilst –

THE BEACON IN THE STORM

Hark, what sombre tones!
  From far billows dying,
  Listen, hollow sighing,
Blent with heavy moans,
  Blent with eerie crying, –
Till a shriller wail
  Bodes new agony . . . –
Through his horn the gale
  Thunders o'er the sea!

Rain in torrents, hark!
  On the low shore yonder
  Billows die in thunder,
'Neath a heaven all-dark;
  While with dread we wonder
Winter should prevail,
  Ere his time to be . . . –
Through his horn the gale,
  Thunders o'er the sea!

Oh! lost mariners!
  While the ship doth founder,
  Through the darkness round her
Toward the shore one nears
  (Ay, the low shore yonder!)

Brawny arms, – how frail! –
   Stretched out helplessly! . . . –
Through his horn the gale
   Thunders o'er the sea!

Oh! rash mariners!
   While the ship's on-driven,
   Sail on sail shrieks, riven
As with tooth or shears.
   Not a star in heaven!
Strife's of none avail!
   Deadly rocks to lee . . . –
Through his horn the gale
   Thunders o'er the sea!

Lo! what sudden light
   'Tis the star beholden,
   Brighter than all golden
Stars that gem the night:
   Torch God fires to embolden
Mariners who hail
   It, while threateningly
Through his horn the gale
   Thunders o'er the sea!

VICTOR HUGO
TRANSLATED BY N. R. TYERMAN

A HURRICANE AT SEA

Slowly a floor rises, almost becomes a wall.
Gently a ceiling slips down, nearly becomes a floor.
A floor with spots that stretch, as on a breathing
animal's hide. It rises again with a soft lurch.

The floor tilts, is curved, appears to be racing north
with a pattern of dents and dips
over slashes of dark. Now there are white lips,
widening on the wall

that stands up suddenly. The ceiling is all
rumpled, snarled, like a wet animal's fur.
The floor hardens, humps up like rock,
the side of a hill too slant to walk.

White teeth are bared where lazy lips swam.
The ceiling is the lid of a box about to slam.
Is this a real floor I walk? It's an angry spine
that shoots up over a chasm of seething

milk – cold, churned, shoving the stern around.
There's the groaning sound
of a caldron about to buckle, maybe break.
A blizzard of glass and lace

shivers over this dodging box.
It glides up the next high hissing alp – halts
on top. But the top turns hollow while the hollow spins.
I run down a slope and feel like twins,

one leg northeast, one west.
The planks pitch leeward, level an instant, then
rear back to a flat, stunned rest.
It's frightening, that vacant moment. I feel

the Floor beneath the floor reel,
while a thickening wilderness is shunted aft, under.
I'm in a bottle becalmed, but a mountain bloats
ahead, ready to thunder

on it. The floor is rushed into the pit.
Maybe there's no bottom to it.
I'm buried in a quarry, locked in a bucking
room – or bottle, or box – near cracking,

that's knocked about in a black,
enormous, heavy, quaking Room.
Is there a bottom to it? I'm glad not to have to know.
Boulders, canyon-high, smash down on the prow,

59

are shattered to snow, and shouldered off somehow.
Tossed out again on top. Topside bounced
like a top, to scoot the bumpy floor . . .
Out there, it's slicked to a plane almost, already,

though chopped with white to the far baseboard.
The ceiling is placing
itself right, getting steadier,
licking itself smooth. The keel

takes the next swollen hills along their backs –
like a little dog gripped
to a galloping horse – slipping
once in a while, but staying on.

QUA CURSUM VENTUS

As ships becalmed at eve, that lay,
  With canvas drooping, side by side,
Two towers of sail at dawn of day
  Are scarce, long leagues apart, descried;

When fell the night, upsprung the breeze,
  And all the darkling hours they plied,
Nor dreamt but each the selfsame seas
  By each was cleaving, side by side:

E'en so – but why the tale reveal
  Of those whom, year by year unchanged,
Brief absence joined anew to feel,
  Astounded, soul from soul estranged?

At dead of night their sails were filled,
  And onward each, rejoicing, steered:
Ah! neither blame; for neither willed
  Or wist what first with dawn appeared.

To veer, how vain! On, onward strain,
  Brave barks! In light, in darkness too,
Through winds and tides, one compass guides:
  To that and your own selves be true.

But, O blithe breeze! and O great seas!
    Though ne'er, that earliest parting past,
On your wide plain they join again,
    Together lead them home at last!

One port, methought, alike they sought,
    One purpose hold, where'er they fare:
O bounding breeze! O rushing seas!
    At last, at last, unite them there!

A CALM AT SEA

Lies a calm along the deep,
　　Like a mirror sleeps the ocean,
And the anxious steersman sees
　　Round him neither stir nor motion.

Not a breath of wind is stirring,
　　Dread the hush as of the grave –
In the weary waste of waters
　　Not the lifting of a wave.

THE EVEN SEA

Meekly the sea
now plods to shore:
white-faced cattle used to their yard,
the waves, with weary knees,
come back from bouldered hills
of high water,

where all the gray, rough day they seethed like bulls,
till the wind laid down its goads
at shift of tide, and sundown
gentled them; with lowered necks
they amble up the beach
as to their stalls.

BALLADS

SIR PATRICK SPENS

The king sits in Dunfermline town,
　　Drinking the blood-red wine:
"O where will I get a skeely skipper,
　　To sail this new ship of mine?"

O up and spake an eldern knight,
　　Sat at the king's right knee:
"Sir Patrick Spens is the best sailor
　　That ever sail'd the sea."

Our king has written a braid letter,
　　And seal'd it with his hand,
And sent it to Sir Patrick Spens,
　　Was walking on the strand.

"To Noroway, to Noroway,
　　To Noroway o'er the faem;
The king's daughter of Noroway,
　　'Tis thou maun bring her hame."

The first word that Sir Patrick read,
　　Sae loud, loud laughèd he;
The neist word that Sir Patrick read,
　　The tear blinded his e'e.

"O wha is this has done this deed,
    And tauld the king o' me,
To send me out at this time of the year
    To sail upon the sea?

"Be it wind, be it weet, be it hail, be it sleet,
    Our ship must sail the faem;
The king's daughter of Noroway,
    'Tis we must fetch her hame."

They hoysed their sails on Monenday morn,
    Wi' a' the speed they may;
They hae landed in Noroway,
    Upon a Wodensday.

They hadna been a week, a week
    In Noroway but twae,
When that the lord o' Noroway
    Began aloud to say:

"Ye Scottishmen spend a' our king's goud,
    And a' our queenis fee!"
"Ye lie, ye lie, ye liars loud,
    Fu' loud I hear ye lie!

"For I brought as much white monie
    As gane my men and me,

And I brought a half fou o' gude red goud
    Out o'er the sea wi' me.

"Make ready, make ready, my merry men a',
    Our gude ship sails the morn":
"Now, ever alake! my master dear,
    I fear a deadly storm!

"I saw the new moon late yestreen,
    Wi' the auld moon in her arm;
And if we gang to sea, master,
    I fear we'll come to harm."

They hadna sailed a league, a league,
    A league but barely three,
When the lift grew dark, and the wind blew loud,
    And gurly grew the sea.

The ankers brak, and the topmasts lap,
    It was sic a deadly storm,
And the waves came o'er the broken ship,
    Till a' her sides were torn.

"O where will I get a gude sailor,
    To take my helm in hand,
Till I get up to the tall topmast,
    To see if I can spy land?"

"O here am I, a sailor gude,
    To take the helm in hand,
Till you go up to the tall topmast,
    But I fear you'll ne'er spy land."

He hadna gane a step, a step,
    A step but barely ane,
When a bout flew out of our goodly ship,
    And the salt sea it came in.

"Gae fetch a web o' the silken claith,
    Another o' the twine,
And wap them into our ship's side,
    And let na the sea come in."

They fetched a web o' the silken claith,
    Another o' the twine,
And they wapped them roun' that gude ship's side,
    But still the sea came in.

O laith, laith were our gude Scots lords
    To weet their cork-heel'd shoon;
But lang or a' the play was play'd,
    They wat their hats aboon.

And mony was the feather-bed
    That flottered on the faem,

And mony was the gude lord's son
    That never mair cam hame.

The ladies wrang their fingers white,
    The maidens tore their hair,
A' for the sake of their true loves,
    For them they'll see nae mair.

O lang, lang may the ladies sit,
    Wi' their fans into their hand,
Before they see Sir Patrick Spens
    Come sailing to the strand.

And lang, lang may the maidens sit,
    Wi' their goud kames in their hair,
A' waiting for their ain dear loves,
    For them they'll see nae mair.

Half owre, half owre to Aberdour
    'Tis fifty fathoms deep,
And there lies gude Sir Patrick Spens,
    Wi' the Scots lords at his feet.

ANONYMOUS

From THE RHYME OF THE ANCIENT MARINER

And thus spake on that ancient man,
The bright-eyed mariner.

"The ship was cheered, the harbour cleared;
Merrily did we drop
Below the kirk, below the hill,
Below the lighthouse top.

"The sun came up upon the left, –
Out of the sea came he;
And he shone bright, and on the right
Went down into the sea.

"Higher and higher every day,
Till over the mast at noon –"
The Wedding-Guest here beat his breast,
For he heard the loud bassoon.

. . . . .

And thus spake on that ancient man,
The bright-eyed Mariner.

"And now the storm-blast came, and he
Was tyrannous and strong:
He struck with his o'ertaking wings,
And chased us south along.

"With sloping masts and dipping prow, –
As who pursued with yell and blow
Still treads the shadow of his foe,
And forward bends his head –
The ship drove fast; loud roared the blast,
And southward aye we fled.

"And now there came both mist and snow;
And it grew wondrous cold;
And ice, mast-high, came floating by,
As green as emerald.

"And through the drifts the snowy clifts
Did send a dismal sheen;
Nor shapes of men nor beasts we ken –
The ice was all between!

"The ice was here, – the ice was there, –
The ice was all around;
It cracked and growled and roared and howled,
Like noises in a swound!

"At length did come an albatross –
Through the fog it came:
As if it had been a Christian soul,
We hailed it in God's name.

"It ate the food it ne'er had eat,
And round and round it flew:
The ice did split, with a thunder-fit;
The helmsman steered us through!

"And a good south wind came up behind, –
The albatross did follow,
And every day, for food or play,
He came to the mariners' hollo.

"In mist or cloud, on mast or shroud,
It perched for vespers nine;
While all the night, through fog-smoke white,
Glimmered the white moonshine."

"God save thee, ancient Mariner,
From the fiends that plague thee thus! –
Why look'st thou so?" – "With my crossbow
I shot the Albatross."

. . . . .

"And I had done a hellish thing,
And it would work 'em woe;
For, all averred, I had killed the bird
That made the breeze to blow.
'Ah, wretch!' said they, 'the bird to slay,
That made the breeze to blow!'"

"The fair breeze blew; the white foam flew;
The furrow fallowed free:
We were the first that ever burst
Into that silent sea!

"Down dropt the breeze; the sails dropt down, –
'Twas sad as sad could be;
And we did speak only to break
The silence of the sea.

"All in a hot and copper sky
The bloody sun, at noon,
Right above the mast did stand,
No bigger than the moon.

"Day after day, day after day
We stuck – nor breath nor motion –
As idle as a painted ship
Upon a painted ocean!

"Water, water everywhere –
And all the boards did shrink!
Water, water everywhere,
Nor any drop to drink!

"The very deep did rot. – O Christ,
That ever this should be!
Yea, slimy things did crawl with legs
Upon the slimy sea!

"About, about in reel and rout
The death fires danced at night, –
The water, like a witch's oils,
Burnt green and blue and white!

"And some in dreams assured were
Of the Spirit that plagued us so;
Nine fathom deep he had followed us
From the land of mist and snow.

"And every tongue, through utter drought,
Was withered at the root;
We could not speak, no more than if
We had been choked with soot."

.   .   .   .   .

"I fear thee, ancient Mariner!
I fear thy skinny hand!
And thou art long and lank, and brown
As is the ribbed sea-sand.

"I fear thee and thy glittering eye,
And thy skinny hand so brown." –
"Fear not, fear not, thou Wedding-Guest!
This body dropt not down.

"Alone, alone! – all, all alone! –
Alone on the wide, wide sea!
And never a saint took pity on
My soul in agony.

"The many men, so beautiful!
And they all dead did lie;
And a thousand-thousand slimy things
Lived on, – and so did I.

"I looked upon the rotting sea,
And drew my eyes away:
I looked upon the rotting deck,
And there the dead men lay."

. . . . .

"An orphan's curse would drag to hell
A spirit from on high;
But, oh, more horrible than that
Is the curse in a dead man's eye!
Seven days, seven nights I saw that curse, –
And yet I could not die."

SAMUEL TAYLOR COLERIDGE   77

SIR HUMPHREY GILBERT

Southward with fleet of ice
  Sailed the corsair Death;
Wild and fast blew the blast,
  And the east-wind was his breath.

His lordly ships of ice
  Glisten in the sun;
On each side, like pennons wide,
  Flashing crystal streamlets run.

His sails of white sea-mist
  Dripped with silver rain;
But where he passed there were cast
  Leaden shadows o'er the main.

Eastward from Campobello
  Sir Humphrey Gilbert sailed;
Three days or more seaward he bore,
  Then, alas! the land-wind failed.

Alas! the land-wind failed,
  And ice-cold grew the night;
And nevermore, on sea or shore,
  Should Sir Humphrey see the light.

He sat upon the deck,
  The Book was in his hand;

"Do not fear! Heaven is as near,"
    He said, "by water as by land!"

In the first watch of the night,
    Without a signal's sound,
Out of the sea, mysteriously,
    The fleet of Death rose all around.

The moon and the evening star
    Were hanging in the shrouds;
Every mast, as it passed,
    Seemed to rake the passing clouds.

They grappled with their prize,
    At midnight black and cold!
As of a rock was the shock;
    Heavily the ground-swell rolled.

Southward through day and dark,
    They drift in close embrace,
With mist and rain, o'er the open main;
    Yet there seems no change of place.

Southward, forever southward,
    They drift through dark and day;
And like a dream, in the Gulf-Stream
    Sinking, vanish all away.

CASABIANCA

The boy stood on the burning deck,
    Whence all but him had fled;
The flame that lit the battle's wreck
    Shone round him o'er the dead.

Yet beautiful and bright he stood,
    As born to rule the storm;
A creature of heroic blood,
    A proud though childlike form.

The flames rolled on; he would not go
    Without his father's word;
That father, faint in death below,
    His voice no longer heard.

He called aloud, "Say, father, say,
    If yet my task be done?"
He knew not that the chieftain lay
    Unconscious of his son.

"Speak, father!" once again he cried,
    "If I may yet be gone!"
And but the booming shots replied,
    And fast the flames rolled on.

Upon his brow he felt their breath,
    And in his waving hair,
And looked from the lone post of death
    In still yet brave despair;

And shouted but once more aloud,
    "My father! must I stay?"
While o'er him fast, through sail and shroud,
    The wreathing fires made way.

They wrapt the ship in splendor wild,
    They caught the flag on high,
And streamed above the gallant child,
    Like banners in the sky.

There came a burst of thunder sound;
    The boy, – Oh! where was *he*?
Ask of the winds, that far around
    With fragments strewed the sea, –

With shroud and mast and pennon fair,
    That well had borne their part, –
But the noblest thing that perished there
    Was that young, faithful heart.

THE WRECK OF THE HESPERUS

It was the schooner Hesperus,
    That sailed the wintry sea;
And the skipper had taken his little daughtèr,
    To bear him company.

Blue were her eyes as the fairy-flax,
    Her cheeks like the dawn of day,
And her bosom white as the hawthorn buds
    That ope in the month of May.

The skipper he stood beside the helm,
    His pipe was in his mouth,
And he watched how the veering flaw did blow
    The smoke now West, now South.

Then up and spake an old Sailòr,
    Had sailed the Spanish Main,
"I pray thee, put into yonder port,
    For I fear a hurricane.

"Last night the moon had a golden ring,
    And to-night no moon we see!"
The skipper he blew a whiff from his pipe,
    And a scornful laugh laughed he.

Colder and colder blew the wind,
  A gale from the North-east;
The snow fell hissing in the brine,
  And the billows frothed like yeast.

Down came the storm, and smote amain,
  The vessel in its strength;
She shuddered and paused, like a frightened steed,
  Then leaped her cable's length.

"Come hither! come hither! my little daughtèr,
  And do not tremble so;
For I can weather the roughest gale,
  That ever wind did blow."

He wrapped her warm in his seaman's coat
  Against the stinging blast;
He cut a rope from a broken spar,
  And bound her to the mast.

"O father! I hear the church-bells ring,
  O say, what may it be?"
" 'Tis a fog-bell on a rock-bound coast!" –
  And he steered for the open sea.

"O father! I hear the sound of guns,
    O say, what may it be?"
"Some ship in distress, that cannot live
    In such an angry sea!"

"O father! I see a gleaming light,
    O say, what may it be?"
But the father answered never a word,
    A frozen corpse was he.

Lashed to the helm, all stiff and stark,
    With his face turned to the skies,
The lantern gleamed through the gleaming snow
    On his fixed and glassy eyes.

Then the maiden clasped her hands and prayed
    That savèd she might be;
And she thought of Christ, who stilled the wave,
    On the Lake of Galilee.

And fast through the midnight dark and drear,
    Through the whistling sleet and snow,
Like a sheeted ghost, the vessel swept
    Towards the reef of Norman's Woe.

And ever the fitful gusts between
  A sound came from the land;
It was the sound of the trampling surf,
  On the rocks and the hard sea-sand.

The breakers were right beneath her bows,
  She drifted a dreary wreck,
And a whooping billow swept the crew
  Like icicles from her deck.

She struck where the white and fleecy waves
  Looked soft as carded wool,
But the cruel rocks, they gored her side
  Like the horns of an angry bull.

Her rattling shrouds, all sheathed in ice,
  With the masts went by the board;
Like a vessel of glass, she stove and sank,
  Ho! ho! the breakers roared!

At daybreak, on the bleak sea-beach,
  A fisherman stood aghast,
To see the form of a maiden fair,
  Lashed close to a drifting mast,

The salt sea was frozen on her breast,
  The salt tears in her eyes;
And he saw her hair, like the brown sea-weed,
  On the billows fall and rise.

Such was the wreck of the Hesperus,
  In the midnight and the snow!
Christ save us all from a death like this
  On the reef of Norman's Woe!

THE PHANTOM SHIP

In Mather's Magnalia Christi,
    Of the old colonial time,
May be found in prose the legend
    That is here set down in rhyme.

A ship sailed from New Haven,
    And the keen and frosty airs,
That filled her sails at parting,
    Were heavy with good men's prayers.

"O Lord! if it be thy pleasure" –
    Thus prayed the old divine –
"To bury our friends in the ocean,
    Take them, for they are thine!"

But Master Lamberton muttered,
    And under his breath said he,
"This ship is so crank and walty,
    I fear our grave she will be!"

And the ships that came from England,
    When the winter months were gone,
Brought no tidings of this vessel
    Nor of Master Lamberton.

This put the people to praying
    That the Lord would let them hear
What in his greater wisdom
    He had done with friends so dear.

And at last their prayers were answered:
    It was in the month of June,
An hour before the sunset
    Of a windy afternoon,

When, steadily steering landward,
    A ship was seen below,
And they knew it was Lamberton, Master,
    Who sailed so long ago.

On she came, with a cloud of canvas,
    Right against the wind that blew,
Until the eye could distinguish
    The faces of the crew.

Then fell her straining topmasts,
    Hanging tangled in the shrouds,
And her sails were loosened and lifted,
    And blown away like clouds.

And the masts, with all their rigging,
    Fell slowly, one by one,
And the hulk dilated and vanished,
    As a sea-mist in the sun!

And the people who saw this marvel
    Each said unto his friend,
That this was the mould of their vessel,
    And thus her tragic end.

And the pastor of the village
    Gave thanks to God in prayer,
That, to quiet their troubled spirits,
    He had sent this Ship of Air.

TRAFALGAR

'Twas at the close of that dark morn
    On which our hero, conquering, died,
That every seaman's heart was torn
    By stripe of sorrow and of pride:

Of pride that one short day should show
    Deeds of eternal splendour done –
Full twenty hostile ensigns low,
    And twenty glorious victories won:

Of grief, the deepest tenderest grief
    That he on every sea and shore –
Their brave, belov'd, unconquer'd chief –
    Should fly his master-flag no more.

Sad was the eve of that great day;
    But sadder and more dire the night,
When human passion clos'd the fray,
    And elements maintain'd the fight.

All shaken in the conflict past,
    The navies fear'd the tempest loud –
The gale that shook the groaning mast,
    The wave that struck the straining shroud.

By passing gleams of sullen light
    The worn and weary seamen view'd
Their blood-gain'd prizes of the fight
    Go foundering from the awful feud.

And oft, as drown'd men's screams were heard,
    And oft, as sank the ships around,
Some British vessel lost they fear'd,
    And mourn'd some British seamen drown'd.

And oft they cried – as memory told
    Of him, so late their darling pride,
But now a bloody corse and cold –
    "Was it for this our Nelson died?"

Through three short days and three long nights,
    They struggl'd 'gainst the gale's stern force,
And sank the trophies of their fights,
    And thought of that dear hero's corse.

But when the fairer morn arose,
    Bright o'er the still tumultuous main;
They saw no wrecks 'cept those of foes,
    No ruin but of France and Spain.

And, victors now of winds and seas,
    Behold thy British vessels brave
Breasting the ocean at their ease,
    Like sea-birds on their native wave.

And now they cried – because they found
    Their conquering fleet in all its pride,
With Spain's and France's hopes aground –
    "It was for this our Nelson died!"

He died with many a hundred bold
    And sterling hearts as ever beat:
But where's the British heart so cold
    That would not die for such a feat?

Yes, by their memories! – by all
    The honours which their tomb surround,
Theirs was the greatest, noblest fall
    That ever mortal courage crown'd!

Then give them each a hero's grave,
    With no weak tears, no woman's sighs;
Theirs was the death-bed of the brave,
    And heroic be their obsequies.

Haul not your colours from on high,
    Still let your flags of victory soar;
Give every pennant to the sky,
    And let your conquering cannon roar –

That every kindling soul may learn
    How to resign its patriot-breath,
And from an honouring country earn
    The triumphs of a hero's death.

ANONYMOUS

SONGS AND
CHANTEYS

From THE TEMPEST

Full fathom five thy father lies;
   Of his bones are coral made;
Those are pearls that were his eyes:
   Nothing of him that doth fade,
But doth suffer a sea-change
Into something rich and strange.
Sea-nymphs hourly ring his knell:
                       Ding-dong.
    Hark! now I hear them –
        Ding-dong, bell!

WILLIAM SHAKESPEARE

WE'LL GO TO SEA NO MORE

Oh blythely shines the bonnie sun
    Upon the isle of May,
And blythely comes the morning tide
    Into St Andrew's Bay.
Then up, gude-man, the breeze is fair,
    And up, my braw bairns three;
There's gold in yonder bonnie boat
    That sails so well the sea!
        When life's last sun goes feebly down
        And death comes to our door,
        When all the world's a dream to us,
        We'll go to sea no more.

I've seen the waves as blue as air,
    I've seen them green as grass;
But I never feared their heaving yet,
    From Grangemouth to the Bass.
I've seen the sea as black as pitch,
    I've seen it white as snow:
But I never feared its foaming yet,
    Though the winds blew high or low.
        When life's last sun goes feebly down
        And death comes to our door,
        When all the world's a dream to us,
        We'll go to sea no more.

I never liked the landsman's life,
    The earth is aye the same;
Give me the ocean for my dower,
    My vessel for my hame.
Give me the fields that no man ploughs,
    The farm that pays no fee:
Give me the bonnie fish, that glance
    So gladly through the sea.
        When life's last sun goes feebly down
        And death comes to our door,
        When all the world's a dream to us,
        We'll go to sea no more.

The sun is up, and round Inchkeith
    The breezes softly blaw;
The gude-man has the lines aboard –
    Awa' my bairns, awa'
An' ye'll be back by gloaming grey,
    An' bright the fire will glow,
An' in your tales and songs we'll tell
    How weel the boat ye row.
        When life's last sun goes feebly down
        And death comes to our door,
        When all the world's a dream to us,
        We'll go to sea no more.

ANONYMOUS

FRANKIE'S TRADE

Old Horn to All Atlantic said:
 (A-hay O! To me O!)
"Now where did Frankie learn his trade?
For he ran me down with a three-reef mains'l."
 (All round the Horn!)

Atlantic answered: – "Not from me!
You better ask the cold North Sea,
For he ran me down under all plain canvas."
 (All round the Horn!)

The North Sea answered: – "He's my man,
For he came to me when he began –
Frankie Drake in an open coaster.
 (All round the Sands!)

"I caught him young and I used him sore,
So you never shall startle Frankie more,
Without capsizing Earth and her waters.
 (All round the Sands!)

"I did not favour him at all.
I made him pull and I made him haul –
And stand his trick with the common sailors.
 (All round the Sands!)

"I froze him stiff and I fogged him blind,
And kicked him home with his road to find
By what he could see in a three-day snowstorm.
    (All round the Sands!)

"I learned him his trade o' winter nights,
'Twixt Mardyk Fort and Dunkirk lights
On a five-knot tide with the forts a-firing.
    (All round the Sands!)

"Before his beard began to shoot,
I showed him the length of the Spaniard's foot –
And I reckon he clapped the boot on it later.
    (All round the Sands!)

"If there's a risk which you can make,
That's worse than he was used to take
Nigh every week in the way of his business;
    (All round the Sands!)

"If there's a trick that you can try,
Which he hasn't met in time gone by,
Not once or twice, but ten times over;
    (All round the Sands!)

"If you can teach him aught that's new,
 (A-hay O! To me O!)
I'll give you Bruges and Niewport too,
And the ten tall churches that stand between 'em,"
 Storm along my gallant Captains!
  (All round the Horn!)

THE DEATH OF
ADMIRAL BENBOW

Come all you sailors bold,
    Lend an ear, lend an ear, –
Come all you sailors bold,
    Lend an ear –
'Tis of our admiral's fame,
Brave Benbow was his name,
How he fought upon the main,
    You shall hear, you shall hear.

Brave Benbow, he set sail,
    For to fight, for to fight, –
Brave Benbow he set sail,
    For to fight –
Brave Benbow he set sail,
With a fine and pleasant gale;
But his captains they turn'd tail
    In a fight, in a fight.

Says Kirby unto Wade,
    "I will run, – I will run!"
Says Kirby unto Wade,
    "I will run!
I value not disgrace
Nor the losing of my place;

No enemies I'll face
    With a gun, with a gun!"

'Twas the *Ruby* and *Noah's Ark*
    Fought the French, fought the French, –
'Twas the *Ruby* and *Noah's Ark*
    Fought the French:
And there was ten in all, –
Poor souls they fought them all,
Nor valu'd them at all,
    Nor their noise, nor their noise.

It was our admiral's lot,
    With chain-shot, with chain-shot, –
It was our admiral's lot,
    With chain-shot:
Our admiral lost his legs,
And to his men he begs –
"Fight on, brave boys," he says –
    "'Tis my lot."

While the surgeon dress'd his wounds,
    Thus said he, thus said he, –
While the surgeon dress'd his wounds,
    Thus said he –
"Let my cradle now in haste
On the quarter-deck be plac'd,

That my enemies be fac'd
    Till I'm dead, till I'm dead."

And there brave Benbow lay,
    Crying out, crying out, –
And there brave Benbow lay,
    Crying out –
"Come, boys, we'll tack once more;
And we'll drive them all ashore, –
I value not a score,
    Nor their noise, nor their noise!"

ANONYMOUS

HEARTS OF OAK

Hearts of oak who wish to try
Your fortunes on the sea,
And Britain's enemies defy,
Come, enter here with me.

Here's fifty pounds bounty, two months' pay,
And leave to go on shore,
With pretty girls to kiss and play,
Can British Tars ask more?

Our ship is stout, and sails like wind,
To chase a hostile foe,
To fight like Britons we're inclin'd
We'll let the Mounseers know,

Our Captain's gen'rous, brave and good,
Of grog we'll have great store,
Of prizes rich we'll sweep the flood,
Can British Tars wish more?

And when, from driving Bourbon's fleet,
Victorious we arrive,
With Music, dance, and jovial treat,
To please our girls we'll strive.

Both Spanish silver and French gold,
We'll count in plenty o'er,
Which we have won, my shipmates bold,
Can British Tars wish more?

DAVEY JONES'S LOCKER

When last honest Jack, of whose fate I now sing,
    Weigh'd anchor, and cast out for Sea,
For he never refus'd, for his Country and King
    To fight, for no lubber was he:
To hand, reef and steer, and bouse ev'ry thing tight
    Full well did he know ev'ry inch,
Tho' the top lifts of sailors the tempest should smite,
    Jack never was known for to flinch.

Aloft from the mast head, one day he espy'd
    Seven sail which appear'd to his view,
Clear the decks, spunge the guns, was instantly cried,
    And each to his station then flew:
And fought until many a noble was slain,
    And silenc'd was every gun,
'Twas there that old English valour was vain,
    For by numbers, alas, they're undone.

Yet think not bold Jack, tho' by Conquest dismay'd,
    Could tamely submit to his fate,
When his country he found he could no longer serve,
    Looking round, he address'd thus each mate;
What's life d'ye see, when our liberty's gone?
    Much nobler it were for to die,
So now for old Davey, then plung'd in the Main –
    E'en the Cherub above heav'd a sigh.

A SONG IN STORM
1914–18

Be well assured that on our side
    The abiding oceans fight,
Though headlong wind and heaping tide
    Make us their sport to-night.
By force of weather, not of war,
    In jeopardy we steer:
Then welcome Fate's discourtesy
    Whereby it shall appear
        How in all time of our distress,
        And our deliverance too,
        The game is more than the player of the game,
        And the ship is more than the crew!

Out of the mist into the mirk
    The glimmering combers roll.
Almost these mindless waters work
    As though they had a soul –
Almost as though they leagued to whelm
    Our flag beneath their green:
Then welcome Fate's discourtesy
    Whereby it shall be seen, etc.

Be well assured, though wave and wind
    Have mightier blows in store,
That we who keep the watch assigned

Must stand to it the more;
And as our streaming bows rebuke
    Each billow's baulked career,
Sing, welcome Fate's discourtesy
    Whereby it is made clear, etc.

No matter though our decks be swept
    And mast and timber crack –
We can make good all loss except
    The loss of turning back.
So, 'twixt these Devils and our deep
    Let courteous trumpets sound,
To welcome Fate's discourtesy
    Whereby it will be found, etc.

Be well assured, though in our power
    Is nothing left to give
But chance and place to meet the hour,
    And leave to strive to live,
Till these dissolve our Order holds,
    Our Service binds us here.
Then welcome Fate's discourtesy
    Whereby it is made clear
        How in all time of our distress,
        As in our triumph too,
        The game is more than the player of the game,
        And the ship is more than the crew!

A PIER-HEAD CHORUS

Oh I'll be chewing salted horse and biting flinty bread,
And dancing with the stars to watch, upon the fo'c's'le
    head,
Hearkening to the bow-wash and the welter of the tread
    Of a thousand tons of clipper running free.

For the tug has got the tow-rope and will take us to
        the Downs,
Her paddles churn the river-wrack to muddy greens
        and browns,
And I have given river-wrack and all the filth of towns
    For the rolling, combing cresters of the sea.

We'll sheet the mizzen-royals home and shimmer down
        the Bay,
The sea-line blue with billows, the land-line blurred
        and grey;
The bow-wash will be piling high and thrashing into
        spray,
    As the hooker's fore-foot tramples down the swell.

She'll log a giddy seventeen and rattle out the reel,
The weight of all the run-out line will be a thing to feel,
As the bacca-quidding shell-back shambles aft to take
        the wheel,
    And the sea-sick little middy strikes the bell.

JOHN MASEFIELD   111

From H.M.S. PINAFORE

I

We sail the ocean blue,
And our saucy ship's a beauty;
We're sober men and true,
And attentive to our duty.
When the balls whistle free
O'er the bright blue sea,
We stand to our guns all day;
When at anchor we ride
On the Portsmouth tide,
We have plenty of time to play.

II

CAPT.   I am the Captain of the *Pinafore*;
ALL   And a right good captain, too!
CAPT.   You're very, very good,
          And be it understood,
     I command a right good crew.
ALL   We're very, very good,
          And be it understood,
     He commands a right good crew.
CAPT.   Though related to a peer,
     I can hand, reef, and steer,
       And ship a selvagee;
     I am never known to quail

	At the fury of a gale,
	And I'm never, never sick at sea!
ALL	What, never?
CAPT.	No, never!
ALL	What, *never*?
CAPT.	Hardly ever!
ALL	He's hardly ever sick at sea!
	Then give three cheers, and one cheer more,
	For the hardy Captain of the *Pinafore*!

CAPT.	I do my best to satisfy you all –
ALL	And with you we're quite content.
CAPT.	You're exceedingly polite,
	And I think it only right
	To return the compliment.
ALL	We're exceedingly polite,
	And he thinks it's only right
	To return the compliment.
CAPT.	Bad language or abuse,
	I never, never use,
	Whatever the emergency;
	Though "Bother it" I may
	Occasionally say,
	I never use a big, big D –
ALL	What, never?

CAPT.	No, never!
ALL	What, *never?*
CAPT.	Hardly ever!
ALL	Hardly ever swears a big, big D –
	Then give three cheers, and one cheer more,
	For the well-bred Captain of the *Pinafore!*

MATELOT

Jean Louis Dominic Pierre Bouchon,
True to the breed that bore him,
Answered the call
That held in thrall
His father's heart before him.
Jean Louis Dominic sailed away
Further than love could find him
Yet through the night
He heard a light
And gentle voice behind him say:

REFRAIN 1
Matelot, Matelot,
Where you go
My thoughts go with you,
Matelot, Matelot,
When you go down to the sea
As you gaze from afar
On the evening star
Wherever you may roam,
You will remember the light
Through the winter night
That guides you safely home.
Though you find

Womenkind
To be frail,
One love cannot fail, my son,
Till our days are done,
Matelot, Matelot,
Where you go
My thoughts go with you,
Matelot, Matelot,
When you go down to the sea.

VERSE 2
Jean Louis Dominic Pierre Bouchon
Journeyed the wide world over,
Lips that he kissed
Could not resist
This loving roving rover.
Jean Louis Dominic right or wrong
Ever pursued a new love,
Till in his brain
There beat a strain
He knew
To be his true love
Song:

REFRAIN 2
Matelot, Matelot,
Where you go

My heart goes with you,
Matelot, Matelot,
When you go down to the sea.
For a year and a day
You may sail away
And have no thought of me,
Yet through the wind and the spray,
You will hear me say
No love was ever free.
You will sigh
When horizons are clear,
Something that is dear
To me
Cannot let me be,
Matelot, Matelot,
Where you go
My heart goes with you,
Matelot, Matelot,
When you go down to the sea.

REFRAIN 3
Matelot, Matelot,
Where you go
My heart will follow,
Matelot, Matelot,
When you go down to the sea.
When there's grief in the sky

And the waves ride high
My heart to yours will say
You may be sure, that I'm true
To my love for you.
Though half the world away,
Never mind
If you find other charms,
Here within my arms
You'll sleep,
Sailor from the deep,
Matelot, Matelot,
Where you go
My heart will follow,
Matelot, Matelot,
When you go down to the sea.

"MY BOUNDING BARK"

My bounding bark, I fly to thee, –
    I'm wearied of the shore;
I long to hail the swelling sea,
    And wander free once more:
A sailor's life of reckless glee,
    That only is the life for me!

I was not born for fashion's slave,
    Or the dull city's strife;
Be mine the spirit-stirring wave,
    The roving sailor's life:
A life of freedom on the sea,
    That only is the life for me!

I was not born for lighted halls,
    Or the gay revel's round;
My music is where Ocean calls,
    And echoing rocks resound:
The wandering sailor's life of glee,
    That only is the life for me!

ANONYMOUS

BLOW THE MAN DOWN

Blow the man down, bullies, blow the man down –
Away-aye, blow the man down!
Blow the man down, bullies, blow him right down –
Give me some time to blow the man down!

Blow him right down from his feet to his crown –
Away-aye, blow the man down!
Blow him right down from his feet to his crown –
Give me some time to blow the man down!

As I was out walking in Paradise Street –
Away-aye, blow the man down!
As I was out walking in Paradise Street –
Give me some time to blow the man down!

A fine handsome girl there I chanced for to meet –
Away-aye, blow the man down!
A fine handsome girl there I chanced for to meet –
Give me some time to blow the man down!

This fine handsome girl then she said unto me –
Away-aye, blow the man down!
This fine handsome girl then she said unto me –
Give me some time to blow the man down!

"There's a spanking full-rigger just ready for sea" –
Away-aye, blow the man down!
"There's a spanking full-rigger just ready for sea" –
Give me some time to blow the man down!

That spanking full-rigger to Melbourne was bound –
Away-aye, blow the man down!
That spanking full-rigger to Melbourne was bound –
Give me some time to blow the man down!

She was very well-manned and very well-found –
Away-aye, blow the man down!
She was very well-manned and very well-found –
Give me some time to blow the man down!

But as soon as that packet was out on the sea –
Away-aye, blow the man down!
But as soon as that packet was out on the sea –
Give me some time to blow the man down!

I'd devilish bad treatment of every degree –
Away-aye, blow the man down!
I'd devilish bad treatment of every degree –
Give me some time to blow the man down!

So I give you this warning, afore we belay –
Away-aye, blow the man down!
So I give you this warning, afore we belay –
Give me some time to blow the man down!

Don't ever take heed now what handsome girls say –
Away-aye, blow the man down!
Don't ever take heed now what spanking girls say –
Give me some time to blow the man down!

DRUNKEN SAILOR

What shall we do with a drunken sailor,
What shall we do with a drunken sailor,
What shall we do with a drunken sailor,
  Early in the morning?
 Way-aye, there she rises,
 Way-aye, there she rises,
 Way-aye, there she rises,
  Early in the morning!

Chuck him in the long-boat till he gets sober,
Chuck him in the long-boat till he gets sober,
Chuck him in the long-boat till he gets sober,
  Early in the morning!
 Way-aye, there she rises,
 Way-aye, there she rises,
 Way-aye, there she rises,
  Early in the morning!

ANTHEM, PRAYER, HYMN

RULE, BRITANNIA

When Britain first at Heaven's command
    Arose from out the azure main,
This was the charter of her land,
    And guardian angels sung the strain:
Rule, Britannia! Britannia rules the waves!
    Britons never shall be slaves.

The nations not so blest as thee
    Must in their turn to tyrants fall,
While thou shalt flourish great and free
    The dread and envy of them all.

Still more majestic shalt thou rise,
    More dreadful from each foreign stroke;
As the loud blast that tears the skies
    Serves but to root thy native oak.

Thee haughty tyrants ne'er shall tame;
    All their attempts to bend thee down
Will but arouse thy generous flame,
    And work their woe and thy renown.

To thee belongs the rural reign;
    Thy cities shall with commerce shine;
All thine shall be the subject main,
    And every shore it circles thine!

The Muses, still with Freedom found,
   Shall to thy happy coast repair;
Blest Isle, with matchless beauty crown'd
   And manly hearts to guard the fair: –
Rule, Britannia! Britannia rules the waves!
   Britons never shall be slaves!

From CARMINA GADELICA

Helmsman:	Blest be the boat.
Crew:	God the Father bless her.
Helmsman:	Blest be the boat.
Crew:	God the Son bless her.
Helmsman:	Blest be the boat.
Crew:	God the Spirit bless her.
All:	God the Father,
	God the Son,
	God the Spirit,
	Bless the boat.
Helmsman:	What can befall you
	And God the Father with you?
Crew:	No harm can befall us.
Helmsman:	What can befall you
	And God the Son with you?
Crew:	No harm can befall us.
Helmsman:	What can befall you
	And God the Spirit with you?
Crew:	No harm can befall us.
All:	God the Father,
	God the Son,
	God the Spirit,
	With us eternally.
Helmsman:	What can cause you anxiety
	And the God of the elements over you?

129

Crew:	No anxiety can be ours.
Helmsman:	What can cause you anxiety
	And the King of the elements over you?
Crew:	No anxiety can be ours.
Helmsman:	What can cause you anxiety
	And the Spirit of the elements over you?
Crew:	No anxiety can be ours.
All:	The God of the elements,
	The King of the elements,
	The Spirit of the elements,
	Close over us,
	Ever eternally.

FATHER MAPPLE'S HYMN
From Moby-Dick

The ribs and terrors in the whale,
   Arched over me a dismal gloom,
While all God's sun-lit waves rolled by,
   And lift me deepening down to doom.

I saw the opening maw of hell,
   With endless pains and sorrows there;
Which none but they that feel can tell –
   Oh, I was plunging to despair.

In black distress, I called my God,
   When I could scarce believe him mine,
He bowed his ear to my complaints –
   No more the whale did me confine.

With speed he flew to my relief,
   As on a radiant dolphin borne;
Awful, yet bright, as lightning shone
   The face of my Deliverer God.

My song for ever shall record
   That terrible, that joyful hour;
I give the glory to my God,
   His all the mercy and the power.

HERMAN MELVILLE

THE SEA RITUAL

Prayer unsaid, and mass unsung,
Deadman's dirge must still be rung:
    Dingle-dong, the dead-bells sound!
    Mermen chant his dirge around!

Wash him bloodless, smooth him fair,
Stretch his limbs, and sleek his hair:
    Dingle-dong, the dead-bells go!
    Mermen swing them to and fro!

In the wormless sands shall he
Feast for no foul gluttons be:
    Dingle-dong, the dead-bells chime!
    Mermen keep the tune and time!

We must with a tombstone brave
Shut the shark from out his grave:
    Dingle-dong, the dead-bells toll!
    Mermen's dirgers ring his knoll!

Such a slab will we lay o'er him
All the dead shall rise before him!
    Dingle-dong, the dead-bells boom!
    Mermen lay him in his tomb!

THE SAILORS' HYMN

Eternal Father, strong to save,
Whose arm doth bind the restless wave,
Who bidd'st the mighty ocean deep
Its own appointed limits keep:
 O hear us, when we cry to thee,
 For those in peril on the sea.

O Saviour, whose almighty word
The winds and waves submissive heard,
Who walkedst on the foaming deep
And calm amidst its rage didst sleep:
 O hear us, when we cry to thee,
 For those in peril on the sea.

O sacred Spirit, who didst brood
Upon the chaos dark and rude,
Who bad'st its angry tumult cease
And gavest light and life and peace:
 O hear us, when we cry to thee,
 For those in peril on the sea.

O Trinity of love and power,
Our brethren shield in danger's hour,
From rock and tempest, fire and foe,
Protect them wheresoe'er they go:
    And ever let there rise to thee
    Glad hymns of praise from land and sea.

SEAFARERS

From PARADISE LOST, BOOK XI

At length a reverend sire among them came,
And of their doings great dislike declar'd,
And testify'd against their ways; he oft
Frequented their assemblies, whereso met,
Triumphs, or festivals, and to them preach'd
Conversion and repentance, as to souls
In prison under judgments imminent:
But all in vain: which when he saw, he ceas'd
Contending, and remov'd his tents far off:
Then from the mountain hewing timber tall,
Began to build a vessel of huge bulk,
Measur'd by cubit, length, and breadth, and height,
Smear'd round with pitch, and in the side a door
Contriv'd, and of provisions laid in large
For man and beast: when lo, a wonder strange!
Of every beast, and bird, and insect small,
Came sevens, and pairs, and enter'd in, as taught
Their order: last the sire and his three sons
With their four wives; and God made fast the door.
Meanwhile the south wind rose, and, with black wings
Wide hovering, all the clouds together drove
From under heaven; the hills to their supply
Vapour, and exhalation dusk and moist,
Sent up amain: and now the thicken'd sky
Like a dark ceiling stood; down rush'd the rain

Impetuous, and continu'd till the earth
No more was seen; the floating vessel swum
Uplifted, and secure with beaked prow
Rode tilting o'er the waves; all dwellings else
Flood overwhelm'd, and them with all their pomp
Deep under water roll'd; sea cover'd sea,
Sea without shore, and in their palaces,
Where luxury late reign'd, sea-monsters whelp'd
And stabled; of mankind, so numerous late,
All left in one small bottom swum imbark'd.

From THE ODYSSEY, BOOK XII

And now arose the morning ray;
Swift to her dome the Goddess held her way.
Then to my mates I measur'd back the plain,
Climb'd the tall bark, and rush'd into the main;
Then bending to the stroke, their oars they drew
To their broad breasts, and swift the galley flew.
Up sprung a brisker breeze; with fresh'ning gales
The friendly Goddess stretch'd the swelling sails;
We drop our oars: at ease the pilot guides:
The vessel light along the level glides.
When rising sad and slow, with pensive look,
Thus to the melancholy train I spoke:

O friends, oh ever partners of my woes,
Attend while I what Heav'n foredooms disclose.
Hear all! Fate hangs o'er all! on you it lies
To live, or perish! to be safe, be wise!

In flow'ry meads the sportive *Sirens* play,
Touch the soft lyre, and tune the vocal lay;
Me, me alone, with fetters firmly bound,
The Gods allow to hear the dangerous sound.
Hear and obey: If freedom I demand,
Be ev'ry fetter strain'd, be added band to band.

While yet I speak the winged galley flies,
And lo! the *Siren* shores like mists arise.
Sunk were at once the winds; the air above,

And waves below, at once forgot to move!
Some Demon calm'd the Air, and smooth'd the deep,
Hush'd the loud winds, and charm'd the waves to sleep.
Now every sail we furl, each oar we ply;
Lash'd by the stroke the frothy waters fly.
The ductile wax with busy hands I mold,
And cleft in fragments, and the fragments roll'd;
Th' aereal region now grew warm with day,
The wax dissolv'd beneath the burning ray;
Then every ear I barr'd against the strain,
And from access of phrenzy lock'd the brain.
Now round the mast my mates the fetters roll'd,
And bound me limb by limb, with fold on fold.
Then bending to the stroke, the active train
Plunge all at once their oars, and cleave the main.

While to the shore the rapid vessel flies,
Our swift approach the *Siren* quire descries;
Celestial music warbles from their tongue,
And thus the sweet deluders tune the song.

O stay, oh pride of *Greece*! *Ulysses* stay!
O cease thy course, and listen to our lay!
Blest is the man ordain'd our voice to hear,
The song instructs the soul, and charms the ear.
Approach! thy soul shall into raptures rise!
Approach! and learn new wisdom from the wise.
We know whate'er the Kings of mighty name
Achiev'd at *Ilion* in the field of fame;

Whate'er beneath the sun's bright journey lies.
O stay, and learn new wisdom from the wise!

Thus the sweet charmers warbled o'er the main;
My soul takes wing to meet the heav'nly strain;
I give the sign, and struggle to be free:
Swift row my mates, and shoot along the sea;
New chains they add, and rapid urge the way,
'Til dying off, the distant sounds decay:
Then scudding swiftly from the dang'rous ground,
The deafen'd ear unlock'd, the chains unbound.

Now all at once tremendous scenes unfold;
Thunder'd the deeps, the smoking billows roll'd!
Tumultuous waves embroil'd the bellowing flood,
All trembling, deafen'd, and aghast we stood!
No more the vessel plow'd the dreadful wave,
Fear seiz'd the mighty, and unnerv'd the brave;
Each dropp'd his oar: But swift from man to man
With look serene I turn'd, and thus began.
O friends! Oh often try'd in adverse storms!
With ills familiar in more dreadful forms!
Deep in the dire *Cyclopean* den you lay,
Yet safe return'd – *Ulysses* led the way.
Learn courage hence! and in my care confide:
Lo! still the same *Ulysses* is your guide!
Attend my words! your oars incessant ply;
Strain ev'ry nerve, and bid the vessel fly.
If from yon justling rocks and wavy war

Jove safety grants; he grants it to your care.
And thou whose guiding hand directs our way,
Pilot, attentive listen and obey!
Bear wide thy course, nor plow those angry waves
Where rolls yon smoke, yon tumbling ocean raves;
Steer by the higher rock: lest whirl'd around
We sink, beneath the circling eddy drown'd.

    While yet I speak, at once their oars they seize,
Stretch to the stroke, and brush the working seas.
Cautious the name of *Scylla* I supprest;
That dreadful sound had chill'd the boldest breast.

    Mean-time, forgetful of the voice divine,
All dreadful bright my limbs in armour shine;
High on the deck I take my dang'rous stand,
Two glitt'ring javelins lighten in my hand;
Prepar'd to whirl the whizzing spear I stay,
'Til the fell fiend arise to seize her prey.
Around the dungeon, studious to behold
The hideous pest, my labouring eyes I roll'd;
In vain! the dismal dungeon dark as night
Veils the dire monster, and confounds the sight.

    Now thro' the rocks, appal'd with deep dismay,
We bend our course, and stem the desp'rate way;
Dire *Scylla* there a scene of horror forms,
And here *Charybdis* fills the deep with storms.
When the tide rushes from her rumbling caves
The rough rock roars; tumultuous boil the waves;

They toss, they foam, a wild confusion raise,
Like waters bubbling o'er the fiery blaze;
Eternal mists obscure th' aereal plain,
And high above the rock she spouts the main:
When in her gulphs the rushing sea subsides,
She drains the ocean with the refluent tides:
The rock rebellows with a thund'ring sound;
Deep, wond'rous deep, below appears the ground.
   Struck with despair, with trembling hearts we
      view'd
The yawning dungeon, and the tumbling flood;
When lo! fierce *Scylla* stoop'd to seize her prey,
Stretch'd her dire jaws and swept six men away;
Chiefs of renown! loud echoing shrieks arise;
I turn, and view them quivering in the skies;
They call, and aid with out-stretch'd arms implore:
In vain they call! those arms are stretch'd no more.
As from some rock that overhangs the flood,
The silent fisher casts th' insidious food,
With fraudful care he waits the finny prize,
And sudden lifts it quivering to the skies:
So the foul monster lifts her prey on high,
So pant the wretches, struggling in the sky,
In the wide dungeon she devours her food,
And the flesh trembles while she churns the blood.
Worn as I am with griefs, with care decay'd;
Never, I never, scene so dire survey'd!

My shiv'ring blood congeal'd forgot to flow,
Aghast I stood, a monument of woe!

TRANSLATED BY ALEXANDER POPE

From ULYSSES

There lies the port; the vessel puffs her sail;
There gloom the dark, broad seas. My mariners,
Souls that have toil'd, and wrought, and thought
    with me, –
That ever with a frolic welcome took
The thunder and the sunshine, and opposed
Free hearts, free foreheads, – you and I are old;
Old age hath yet his honour and his toil.
Death closes all; but something ere the end,
Some work of noble note, may yet be done,
Not unbecoming men that strove with Gods.
The lights begin to twinkle from the rocks;
The long day wanes; the slow moon climbs; the deep
Moans round with many voices. Come, my friends.
'Tis not too late to seek a newer world.
Push off, and sitting well in order smite
The sounding furrows; for my purpose holds
To sail beyond the sunset, and the baths
Of all the western stars, until I die.
It may be that the gulfs will wash us down;
It may be we shall touch the Happy Isles,
And see the great Achilles, whom we knew.
Tho' much is taken, much abides; and tho'
We are not now that strength which in old days
Moved earth and heaven, that which we are, we are, –

One equal temper of heroic hearts
Made weak by time and fate, but strong in will
To strive, to seek, to find, and not to yield.

ITHAKA

As you set out for Ithaka
hope the voyage is a long one,
full of adventure, full of discovery.
Laistrygonians and Cyclops,
angry Poseidon – don't be afraid of them:
you'll never find things like that on your way
as long as you keep your thoughts raised high,
as long as a rare excitement
stirs your spirit and your body.
Laistrygonians and Cyclops,
wild Poseidon – you won't encounter them
unless you bring them along inside your soul,
unless your soul sets them up in front of you.

Hope the voyage is a long one.
May there be many a summer morning when,
with what pleasure, what joy,
you come into harbors seen for the first time;
may you stop at Phoenician trading stations
to buy fine things,
mother of pearl and coral, amber and ebony,
sensual perfume of every kind –
as many sensual perfumes as you can;
and may you visit many Egyptian cities
to gather stores of knowledge from their scholars.

Keep Ithaka always in your mind.
Arriving there is what you are destined for.
But do not hurry the journey at all.
Better if it lasts for years,
so you are old by the time you reach the island,
wealthy with all you have gained on the way,
not expecting Ithaka to make you rich.

Ithaka gave you the marvelous journey.
Without her you would not have set out.
She has nothing left to give you now.

And if you find her poor, Ithaka won't have fooled you.
Wise as you will have become, so full of experience,
you will have understood by then what
        these Ithakas mean.

SONG OF THE ARGONAUTS

O bitter sea, tumultuous sea,
Full many an ill is wrought by thee! –
Unto the wasters of the land
Thou holdest out thy wrinkled hand;
And when they leave the conquered town,
Whose black smoke makes thy surges brown,
Driven betwixt thee and the sun,
As the long day of blood is done,
From many a league of glittering waves
Thou smilest on them and their slaves.

Now, therefore, O thou bitter sea,
With no long words we pray to thee,
But ask thee, hast thou felt before
Such strokes of the long ashen oar?
And hast thou yet seen such a prow
Thy rich and niggard waters plough?

Nor yet, O sea, shalt thou be cursed,
If at thy hands we gain the worst,
And, wrapt in water, roll about
Blind-eyed, unheeding song or shout,
Within thine eddies far from shore,
Warmed by no sunlight any more.

Therefore, indeed, we joy in thee,
And praise thy greatness, and will we
Take at thy hands both good and ill,

Yea, what thou wilt, and praise thee still,
Enduring not to sit at home,
And wait until the last days come,
When we no more may care to hold
White bosoms under crowns of gold,
And our dulled hearts no longer are
Stirred by the clangorous noise of war,
And hope within our souls is dead,
And no joy is remembered.

   So, if thou hast a mind to slay,
Fair prize thou hast of us today;
And if thou hast a mind to save,
Great praise and honour shalt thou have;
But whatso thou wilt do with us,
Our end shall not be piteous,
Because our memories shall live
When folk forget the way to drive
The black keel through the heaped-up sea,
And half dried up thy waters be.

THE SEAFARER

A song I sing of my sea-adventure,
The strain of peril, the stress of toil,
Which oft I endured in anguish of spirit
Through weary hours of aching woe.
My bark was swept by the breaking seas;
Bitter the watch from the bow by night
As my ship drove on within sound of the rocks.
My feet were numb with the nipping cold,
Hunger sapped a sea-weary spirit,
And care weighed heavy upon my heart.
Little the land-lubber, safe on shore,
Knows what I've suffered in icy seas
Wretched and worn by the winter storms,
Hung with icicles, stung by hail,
Lonely and friendless and far from home.
In my ears no sound but the roar of the sea,
The icy combers, the cry of the swan;
In place of the mead-hall and laughter of men
My only singing the sea-mew's call,
The scream of the gannet, the shriek of the gull;
Through the wail of the wild gale beating the bluffs
The piercing cry of the ice-coated petrel,
The storm-drenched eagle's echoing scream.
In all my wretchedness, weary and lone,
I had no comfort of comrade or kin.

Little indeed can he credit, whose town-life
Pleasantly passes in feasting and joy,
Sheltered from peril, what weary pain
Often I've suffered in foreign seas.
Night shades darkened with driving snow
From the freezing north, and the bonds of frost
Firm-locked the land, while falling hail,
Coldest of kernels, encrusted earth.
Yet still, even now, my spirit within me
Drives me seaward to sail the deep,
To ride the long swell of the salt sea-wave.
Never a day but my heart's desire
Would launch me forth on the long sea-path,
Fain of far harbors and foreign shores.
Yet lives no man so lordly of mood,
So eager in giving, so ardent in youth,
So bold in his deeds, or so dear to his lord,
Who is free from dread in his far sea-travel,
Or fear of God's purpose and plan for his fate.
The beat of the harp, and bestowal of treasure,
The love of woman, and worldly hope,
Nor other interest can hold his heart
Save only the sweep of the surging billows;
His heart is haunted by love of the sea.
Trees are budding and towns are fair,
Meadows kindle and all life quickens,
All things hasten the eager-hearted,

Who joyeth therein, to journey afar,
Turning seaward to distant shores.
The cuckoo stirs him with plaintive call,
The herald of summer, with mournful song,
Foretelling the sorrow that stabs the heart.
Who liveth in luxury, little he knows
What woe men endure in exile's doom.
Yet still, even now, my desire outreaches,
My spirit soars over tracts of sea,
O'er the home of the whale, and the world's expanse.
Eager, desirous, the lone sprite returneth;
It cries in my ears and it calls to my heart
To launch where the whales plough their paths
        through the deep.

ANONYMOUS, ANGLO-SAXON   153
TRANSLATED BY CHARLES W. KENNEDY

COLUMBUS

Behind him lay the gray Azores,
    Behind the Gates of Hercules;
Before him not the ghost of shores,
    Before him only shoreless seas.
The good mate said: "Now must we pray,
    For lo! the very stars are gone.
Brave Admiral, speak, what shall I say?"
    "Why, say, 'Sail on! sail on! and on!' "

"My men grow mutinous day by day;
    My men grow ghastly wan and weak."
The stout mate thought of home; a spray
    Of salt wave washed his swarthy cheek.
"What shall I say, brave Admiral, say,
    If we sight naught but seas at dawn?"
"Why, you shall say at break of day,
    'Sail on! sail on! sail on! and on!' "

They sailed and sailed, as winds might blow,
    Until at last the blanched mate said:
"Why, now not even God would know
    Should I and all my men fall dead.
These very winds forget their way,
    For God from these dread seas is gone.
Now speak, brave Admiral, speak and say" –
    He said: "Sail on! sail on! and on!"

They sailed. They sailed. Then spake the mate:
   "This mad sea shows his teeth tonight.
He curls his lip, he lies in wait,
   With lifted teeth, as if to bite!
Brave Admiral, say but one good word:
   What shall we do when hope is gone?"
The words leapt like a leaping sword:
   "Sail on! sail on! sail on! and on!"

Then, pale and worn, he kept his deck,
   And peered through darkness. Ah, that night
Of all dark nights! And then a speck —
   A light! A light! A light! A light!
It grew, a starlit flag unfurled!
   It grew to be Time's burst of dawn.
He gained a world; he gave that world
   Its grandest lesson: "On! sail on!"

THE PIRATE

O'er the glad waters of the dark-blue sea,
Our thoughts as boundless, and our souls as free,
Far as the breeze can bear, the billows foam,
Survey our empire and behold our home!
These are our realms, no limit to our sway –
Our flag the sceptre all who meet obey.
Ours the wild life, in tumult still to range
From toil to rest, and joy in every change.
Oh! who can tell? Not thou, luxurious slave,
Whose soul would sicken o'er the heaving wave!
Not thou, vain lord of wantonness and ease!
Whose slumber soothes not, pleasure cannot please.
Oh! who can tell? – save he whose heart hath tried,
And danced in triumph o'er the waters wide;
Th' exulting sense, the pulse's maddening play,
That thrills the wanderer of this trackless way;
That for itself can woo th' approaching fight,
And turn what some deem danger to delight;
That seeks what cravens shun with more than zeal,
And where the feebler faint, can only feel –
Feel to the rising bosom's inmost core,
Its hope awaken and its spirits soar!
No dread of death – if with us die our foes –
Save that it seems e'en duller than repose:
Come when it will – we snatch the life of life;

When lost – what recks it, by disease or strife?
Let him who crawls, enamoured of decay,
Cling to his couch, and sicken years away;
Heave his thick breath, and shake his palsièd head;
Ours – the fresh turf, and not the feverish bed.
While gasp by gasp he falters forth his soul;
Ours with one pang, one bound, escapes control.
His corse may boast its urn and narrow cave,
And they who loathed his life may gild his grave.
Ours are the tears, though few, sincerely shed,
When Ocean shrouds and sepulchres our dead.
For us, e'en banquets fond regret supply
In the red cup that drowns our memory;
And the brief epitaph in danger's day,
When those who win at last divide the prey,
And cry, Remembrance saddening o'er each brow:
"How had the brave who fell exulted now!"

OLD IRONSIDES

Ay, tear her tattered ensign down!
   Long has it waved on high,
And many an eye has danced to see
   That banner in the sky;
Beneath it rung the battle shout,
   And burst the cannon's roar; –
The meteor of the ocean air
   Shall sweep the clouds no more!

Her deck, once red with heroes' blood
   Where knelt the vanquished foe,
When winds were hurrying o'er the flood
   And waves were white below,
No more shall feel the victor's tread,
   Or know the conquered knee; –
The harpies of the shore shall pluck
   The eagle of the sea!

O better that her shattered hulk
   Should sink beneath the wave;
Her thunders shook the mighty deep,
   And there should be her grave;
Nail to the mast her holy flag,
   Set every thread-bare sail,
And give her to the god of storms, –
   The lightning and the gale!

SEAFARER

And learn O voyager to walk
The roll of earth, the pitch and fall
That swings across these trees those stars:
That swings the sunlight up the wall.

And learn upon these narrow beds
To sleep in spite of sea, in spite
Of sound the rushing planet makes:
And learn to sleep against this ground.

WRECKS AT SEA

THE SHIPWRECK

The tale is different if even a single breath
Escapes to tell it. The return itself
Says survival is possible. And words made to carry
In quiet the burden, the isolation
Of dust, and that fail even so,
Though they shudder still, must shrink the great head
Of elemental violence, the vast eyes
Called blind looking into the ends of darkness,
The mouth deafening understanding with its one
All-wise syllable, into a shrivelled
History that the dry-shod may hold
In the palms of their hands. They had her
Under jib and reefed mizzen, and in the dark
Were fairly sure where they were, and with sea-room,
And it seemed to be slacking a little, until
Just before three they struck. Heard
It come home, hollow in the hearts of them,
And only then heard the bell ringing, telling them
It had been ringing there always telling them
That there it would strike home, hollow, in
The hearts of them. Only then heard it
Over the sunlight, the dozing creak
Of the moorings, the bleaching quay, the heat,
The coiled ropes on the quay the day they would sail
And the day before, and across the water blue

As a sky through the heat beyond
The coils, the coils, with their shadows coiled
Inside them. And it sprang upon them dark,
Bitter, and heavy with sound. They began to go
To pieces at once under the waves' hammer.
Sick at heart since that first stroke, they moved
Nevertheless as they had learned always to move
When it should come, not weighing hope against
The weight of the water, yet knowing that no breath
Would escape to betray what they underwent then.
Dazed too, incredulous, that it had come,
That they could recognize it. It was too familiar,
And they in the press of it, therefore, as though
In a drifting dream. But it bore in upon them
Bursting slowly inside them where they had
Coiled it down, coiled it down: this sea, it was
Blind, yes, as they had said, and treacherous –
They had used their own traits to character it –
    but without
Accident in its wildness, in its rage,
Utterly and from the beginning without
Error. And to some it seemed that the waves
Grew gentle, spared them, while they died
    of that knowledge.

THE CONVERGENCE OF THE TWAIN
Lines on the loss of the "Titanic"

I

In a solitude of the sea
Deep from human vanity,
And the Pride of Life that planned her, stilly couches she.

II

Steel chambers, late the pyres
Of her salamandrine fires,
Cold currents thrid, and turn to rhythmic tidal lyres.

III

Over the mirrors meant
To glass the opulent
The sea-worm crawls – grotesque, slimed, dumb,
indifferent.

IV

Jewels in joy designed
To ravish the sensuous mind
Lie lightless, all their sparkles bleared and black
and blind.

V

Dim moon-eyed fishes near
Gaze at the gilded gear
And query: "What does this vaingloriousness
down here?" . . .

VI

Well: while was fashioning
This creature of cleaving wing,
The Immanent Will that stirs and urges everything

VII

Prepared a sinister mate
For her – so gaily great –
A Shape of Ice, for the time far and dissociate.

VIII

And as the smart ship grew
In stature, grace, and hue,
In shadowy silent distance grew the Iceberg too.

IX

Alien they seemed to be!
No mortal eye could see
The intimate welding of their later history,

X

Or sign that they were bent
By paths coincident
On being anon twin halves of one august event,

XI

Till the Spinner of the Years
Said "Now!" And each one hears
And consummation comes, and jars two hemispheres.

THE QUAKER GRAVEYARD
IN NANTUCKET
For Warren Winslow, Dead at Sea

Let man have dominion over the fishes of the sea and the
fowls of the air and the beasts and the whole earth, and every
creeping creature that moveth upon the earth.

I

A brackish reach of shoal off Madaket, –
The sea was still breaking violently and night
Had steamed into our North Atlantic Fleet,
When the drowned sailor clutched the drag-net. Light
Flashed from his matted head and marble feet,
He grappled at the net
With the coiled, hurdling muscles of his thighs:
The corpse was bloodless, a botch of reds and whites,
Its open, staring eyes
Were lustreless dead-lights
Or cabin-windows on a stranded hulk
Heavy with sand. We weight the body, close
Its eyes and heave it seaward whence it came,
Where the heel-headed dogfish barks its nose
On Ahab's void and forehead; and the name
Is blocked in yellow chalk.
Sailors, who pitch this portent at the sea
Where dreadnaughts shall confess
Its hell-bent deity,

When you are powerless
To sand-bag this Atlantic bulwark, faced
By the earth-shaker, green, unwearied, chaste
In his steel scales: ask for no Orphean lute
To pluck life back. The guns of the steeled fleet
Recoil and then repeat
The hoarse salute.

II

Whenever winds are moving and their breath
Heaves at the roped-in bulwarks of this pier,
The terns and sea-gulls tremble at your death
In these home-waters. Sailor, can you hear
The Pequod's sea wings, beating landward, fall
Headlong and break on our Atlantic wall
Off 'Sconset, where the yawning S-boats splash
The bellbuoy, with ballooning spinnakers,
As the entangled, screeching mainsheet clears
The blocks: off Madaket, where lubbers lash
The heavy surf and throw their long lead squids
For blue-fish? Sea-gulls blink their heavy lids
Seaward. The winds' wings beat upon the stones,
Cousin, and scream for you and the claws rush
At the sea's throat and wring it in the slush
Of this old Quaker graveyard where the bones
Cry out in the long night for the hurt beast
Bobbing by Ahab's whaleboats in the East.

III

All you recovered from Poseidon died
With you, my cousin, and the harrowed brine
Is fruitless on the blue beard of the god,
Stretching beyond us to the castles in Spain,
Nantucket's westward haven. To Cape Cod
Guns, cradled on the tide,
Blast the eelgrass about a waterclock
Of bilge and backwash, roil the salt and sand
Lashing earth's scaffold, rock
Our warships in the hand
Of the great God, where time's contrition blues
Whatever it was these Quaker sailors lost
In the mad scramble of their lives. They died
When time was open-eyed,
Wooden and childish; only bones abide
There, in the nowhere, where their boats were tossed
Sky-high, where mariners had fabled news
Of IS, the whited monster. What it cost
Them is their secret. In the sperm-whale's slick
I see the Quakers drown and hear their cry:
"If God himself had not been on our side,
If God himself had not been on our side,
When the Atlantic rose against us, why,
Then it had swallowed us up quick."

This is the end of the whaleroad and the whale
Who spewed Nantucket bones on the thrashed swell
And stirred the troubled waters to whirlpools
To send the Pequod packing off to hell:
This is the end of them, three-quarters fools,
Snatching at straws to sail
Seaward and seaward on the turntail whale,
Spouting out blood and water as it rolls,
Sick as a dog to these Atlantic shoals:
Clamavimus, O depths. Let the sea-gulls wail

For water, for the deep where the high tide
Mutters to its hurt self, mutters and ebbs.
Waves wallow in their wash, go out and out,
Leave only the death-rattle of the crabs,
The beach increasing, its enormous snout
Sucking the ocean's side.
This is the end of running on the waves;
We are poured out like water. Who will dance
The mast-lashed master of the Leviathans
Up from this field of Quakers in their unstoned graves?

V

When the whale's viscera go and the roll
Of its corruption overruns this world
Beyond tree-swept Nantucket and Wood's Hole

And Martha's Vineyard, Sailor, will your sword
Whistle and fall and sink into the fat?
In the great ash-pit of Jehoshaphat
The bones cry for the blood of the white whale,
The fat flukes arch and whack about its ears,
The death-lance churns into the sanctuary, tears
The gun-blue swingle, heaving like a flail,
And hacks the coiling life out: it works and drags
And rips the sperm-whale's midriff into rags,
Gobbets of blubber spill to wind and weather,
Sailor, and gulls go round the stoven timbers
Where the morning stars sing out together
And thunder shakes the white surf and dismembers
The red flag hammered in the mast-head. Hide
Our steel, Jonas Messias, in Thy side.

VI

Our Lady of Walsingham
There once the penitents took off their shoes
And then walked barefoot the remaining mile;
And the small trees, a stream and hedgerows file
Slowly along the munching English lane,
Like cows to the old shrine, until you lose
Track of your dragging pain.
The stream flows down under the druid tree,
Shiloah's whirlpools gurgle and make glad
The castle of God. Sailor, you were glad

And whistled Sion by that stream. But see:
Our Lady, too small for her canopy,
Sits near the altar. There's no comeliness
At all or charm in that expressionless
Face with its heavy eyelids. As before,
This face, for centuries a memory,
Non est species, neque decor,
Expressionless, expresses God: it goes
Past castled Sion. She knows what God knows,
Not Calvary's Cross nor crib at Bethlehem
Now, and the world shall come to Walsingham.

VII

The empty winds are creaking and the oak
Splatters and splatters on the cenotaph,
The boughs are trembling and a gaff
Bobs on the untimely stroke
Of the greased wash exploding on a shoal-bell
In the old mouth of the Atlantic. It's well;
Atlantic, you are fouled with the blue sailors,
Sea-monsters, upward angel, downward fish:
Unmarried and corroding, spare of flesh
Mart once of supercilious, wing'd clippers,
Atlantic, where your bell-trap guts its spoil
You could cut the brackish winds with a knife
Here in Nantucket, and cast up the time
When the Lord God formed man from the sea's slime

And breathed into his face the breath of life,
And blue-lung'd combers lumbered to the kill.
The Lord survives the rainbow of His will.

THE WRECK OF THE THRESHER
Lost at sea, April 10, 1963

I stand on the ledge where rock runs into the river
As the night turns brackish with morning, and mourn
    the drowned.
Here the sea is diluted with river; I watch it slaver
Like a dog curing of rabies. Its ravening over,
Lickspittle ocean nuzzles the dry ground.
(But the dream that woke me was worse
    than the sea's gray
Slip-slap; there are no such sounds by day.)

This crushing of people is something we live with.
Daily, by unaccountable whim
Or caught up in some harebrained scheme of death,
Tangled in cars, dropped from the sky, in flame,
Men and women break the pledge of breath:
And now under water, gone all jetsam and small
In the pressure of oceans collected, a squad of
    brave men in a hull.

(Why can't our dreams be content with the
    terrible facts?
The only animal cursed with responsible sleep,
We trace disaster always to our own acts.
I met a monstrous self trapped in the black deep:

All these years, he smiled, *I've drilled at sea*
For this crush of water. Then he saved only me.)

We invest ships with life. Look at a harbor
At first light: with better grace than men
In their movements the vessels run to their labors
Working the fields that the tide has made green again;
Their beauty is womanly, they are named for ladies
      and queens,
Although by a wise superstition these are called
After fish, the finned boats, silent and submarine.
The crushing of any ship has always been held
In dread, like a house burned or a great tree felled.

I think of how sailors laugh, as if cold and wet
And dark and lost were their private, funny derision
And I can judge then what dark compression
Astonishes them now, their sunken faces set
Unsmiling, where the currents sluice to and fro
And without humor, somewhere northeast of
      here and below.

(*Sea-brothers, I lower you the ingenuity of dreams,*
Strange lungs and bells to escape in; let me stay aboard last —
We amend our dreams in half-sleep. Then it seems
Easy to talk to the severe dead and explain the past.
Now they are saying, ***Do not be ashamed to stay alive,***

You have dreamt nothing that we do not forgive.
And gentlier, *Study something deeper than yourselves,*
As, how the heart, when it turns diver, delves and saves.)

Whether we give assent to this or rage
Is a question of temperament and does not matter.
Some will has been done past our understanding,
Past our guilt surely, equal to our fears.
Dullards, we are set again to the cryptic blank page
Where the sea schools us with terrible water.
The noise of a boat breaking up and its men is in
      our ears.
The bottom here is too far down for our sounding;
The ocean was salt before we crawled to tears.

LEGENDS

From RICHARD III

Lord, lord! methought what pain it was to drown;
What dreadful noise of water in mine ears!
What sights of ugly death within mine eyes!
Methought I saw a thousand fearful wracks;
A thousand men that fishes gnaw'd upon;
Wedges of gold, great anchors, heaps of pearl,
Inestimable stones, unvalu'd jewels,
All scattered in the bottom of the sea.
Some lay in dead men's skulls; and in those holes
Where eyes did once inhabit, there were crept
As 'twere in scorn of eyes, reflecting gems,
That woo'd the slimy bottom of the deep,
And mocked the dead bones that lay scatter'd by.

WILLIAM SHAKESPEARE   179

THE WORLD BELOW THE BRINE

The world below the brine;
Forests at the bottom of the sea – the branches
    and leaves,
Sea lettuce, vast lichens, strange flowers and seeds –
    the thick tangle, the openings, and the pink turf,
Different colors, pale gray and green, purple, white
    and gold – the play of light through the water,
Dumb swimmers there among the rocks – coral,
    gluten, grass, rushes – and the aliment of the
    swimmers,
Sluggish existences grazing there, suspended,
    or slowly crawling close to the bottom,
The sperm whale at the surface, blowing air and spray,
    or disporting with his flukes,
The leaden-eyed shark, the walrus, the turtle, the hairy
    sea leopard, and the sting ray;
Passions there – wars, pursuits, tribes – sight in those
    ocean depths – breathing that thick-breathing air,
    as so many do;
The change thence to the sight here, and to the subtle
    air breathed by beings like us, who walk
    this sphere;
The change onward from ours, to that of beings
    who walk other spheres.

IN PRAISE OF NEPTUNE

Of Neptune's empire let us sing,
At whose command the waves obey;
To whom the rivers tribute pay,
Down the high mountains sliding;
To whom the scaly nation yields
Homage for the crystal fields
    Wherein they dwell;
And every sea-god pays a gem
Yearly out of his watery cell,
To deck great Neptune's diadem.

The Tritons dancing in a ring,
Before his palace gates do make
The water with their echo quake,
Like the great thunder sounding:
The sea-nymphs chant their accents shrill,
And the Sirens taught to kill
    With their sweet voice,
Make every echoing rock reply,
Unto their gentle murmuring noise,
The praise of Neptune's empery.

THOMAS CAMPION   181

LEVIATHAN

This is the black sea-brute bulling through wave-wrack,
Ancient as ocean's shifting hills, who in sea-toils
Travelling, who furrowing the salt acres
Heavily, his wake hoary behind him,
Shoulders spouting, the fist of his forehead
Over wastes gray-green crashing,
      among horses unbroken
From bellowing fields, past bone-wreck of vessels,
Tide-ruin, wash of lost bodies bobbing
No longer sought for, and islands of ice gleaming,
Who ravening the rank flood, wave-marshalling,
Overmastering the dark sea-marches, finds home
And harvest. Frightening to foolhardiest
Mariners, his size were difficult to describe:
The hulk of him is like hills heaving,
Dark, yet as crags of drift-ice, crowns cracking
      in thunder,
Like land's self by night black-looming, surf churning
      and trailing
Along his shores' rushing, shoal-water boding
About the dark of his jaws; and who should moor at
      his edge
And fare on afoot would find gates of no gardens,
But the hill of dark underfoot diving,
Closing overhead, the cold deep, and drowning.

He is called Leviathan, and named for rolling,
First created he was of all creatures,
He has held Jonah three days and nights,
He is that curling serpent that in ocean is,
Sea-fright he is, and the shadow under the earth.
Days there are, nonetheless,when he lies
Like an angel, although a lost angel
On the waste's unease, no eye of man moving,
Bird hovering, fish flashing, creature whatever
Who after him came to herit earth's emptiness.
Froth at flanks seething soothes to stillness,
Waits; with one eye he watches
Dark of night sinking last, with one eye dayrise
As at first over foaming pastures. He makes no cry
Though that light is a breath. The sea curling,
Star-climbed, wind-combed, cumbered with itself still
As at first it was, is the hand not yet contented
Of the Creator. And he waits for the world to begin.

W. S. MERWIN

THE MERMAID

I

Who would be
A mermaid fair,
Singing alone,
Combing her hair
Under the sea,
In a golden curl
With a comb of pearl,
On a throne?

II

I would be a mermaid fair;
I would sing to myself the whole of the day;
With a comb of pearl I would comb my hair;
And still as I combed I would sing and say,
"Who is it loves me? who loves not me?"
I would comb my hair till my ringlets would fall
    Low adown, low adown,
From under my starry sea-bud crown
    Low adown and around,
And I should look like a fountain of gold
    Springing alone
  With a shrill inner sound,
    Over the throne
In the midst of the hall;

Till that great sea-snake under the sea
From his coiled sleeps in the central deeps
Would slowly trail himself sevenfold
Round the hall where I sate, and look in at the gate
With his large calm eyes for the love of me.
And all the mermen under the sea
Would feel their immortality
Die in their hearts for the love of me.

III

But at night I would wander away, away,
 I would fling on each side my low-flowing locks,
And lightly vault from the throne and play
 With the mermen in and out of the rocks;
We would run to and fro, and hide and seek,
 On the broad sea-wolds in the crimson shells,
 Whose silvery spikes are nighest the sea.
But if any came near I would call, and shriek,
And adown the steep like a wave I would leap
 From the diamond-ledges that jut from the dells;
For I would not be kissed by all who would list,
Of the bold merry mermen under the sea;
They would sue me, and woo me, and flatter me,
In the purple twilights under the sea;
But the king of them all would carry me,
Woo me, and win me, and marry me,
In the branching jaspers under the sea;

Then all the dry pied things that be
In the hueless mosses under the sea
Would curl round my silver feet silently,
All looking up for the love of me.
And if I should carol aloud, from aloft
All things that are forked, and horned, and soft
Would lean out from the hollow sphere of the sea,
All looking down for the love of me.

SEA LULLABY

The old moon is tarnished
With smoke of the flood,
The dead leaves are varnished
With colour like blood,

A treacherous smiler
With teeth white as milk,
A savage beguiler
In sheathings of silk,

The sea creeps to pillage,
She leaps on her prey;
A child of the village
Was murdered today.

She came up to meet him
In a smooth golden cloak,
She choked him and beat him
To death, for a joke.

Her bright locks were tangled,
She shouted for joy,
With one hand she strangled
A strong little boy.

Now in silence she lingers
Beside him all night
To wash her long fingers
In silvery light.

ANNABEL LEE

It was many and many a year ago,
    In a kingdom by the sea,
That a maiden there lived whom you may know
    By the name of Annabel Lee;
And this maiden she lived with no other thought
    Than to love and be loved by me.

I was a child and she was a child,
    In this kingdom by the sea,
But we loved with a love that was more than love,
    I and my Annabel Lee;
With a love that the wingèd seraphs of heaven
    Coveted her and me.

And this was the reason that, long ago,
    In this kingdom by the sea,
A wind blew out of a cloud, chilling
    My beautiful Annabel Lee;
So that her highborn kinsmen came
    And bore her away from me,
To shut her up in a sepulchre
    In this kingdom by the sea.

The angels, not half so happy in heaven,
    Went envying her and me;

Yes! that was the reason (as all men know,
  In this kingdom by the sea)
That the wind came out of the cloud by night,
  Chilling and killing my Annabel Lee.

But our love it was stronger by far than the love
  Of those who were older than we,
  Of many far wiser than we;
And neither the angels in heaven above,
  Nor the demons down under the sea,
Can ever dissever my soul from the soul
  Of the beautiful Annabel Lee:

For the moon never beams, without bringing me
    dreams
  Of the beautiful Annabel Lee;
And the stars never rise, but I feel the bright eyes
  Of the beautiful Annabel Lee;
And so, all the night-tide, I lie down by the side
Of my darling – my darling – my life and my bride,
  In her sepulchre there by the sea,
  In her tomb by the sounding sea.

THE CITY IN THE SEA

Lo! Death has reared himself a throne
In a strange city lying alone
Far down within the dim West,
Where the good and the bad and the worst and the best
Have gone to their eternal rest.
There shrines and palaces and towers
(Time-eaten towers that tremble not!)
Resemble nothing that is ours.
Around, by lifting winds forgot,
Resigned, beneath the sky
The melancholy waters lie.

No rays from the holy heaven come down
On the long night-time of that town;
But light from out the lurid sea
Streams up the turrets silently –
Gleams up the pinnacles far and free –
Up domes – up spires – up kingly halls –

Up fanes – up Babylon-like walls –
Up shadowy long-forgotten bowers
Of sculptured ivy and stone flowers –
Up many and many a marvellous shrine
Whose wreathed friezes intertwine
The viol, the violet, and the vine.

Resignedly beneath the sky
The melancholy waters lie.
So blend the turret and shadows there
That all seem pendulous in air,
While from a proud tower in the town
Death looks gigantically down.

There open fanes and gaping graves
Yawn level with the luminous waves;
But not the riches there that lie
In each idol's diamond eye –
Not the gaily-jewelled dead
Tempt the waters from their bed;
For no ripples curl, alas!
Along that wilderness of glass –
No swellings tell that winds may be
Upon some far-off happier sea –
No heavings hint that winds have been
On seas less hideously serene.

But lo, a stir is in the air!
The wave – there is a movement there!
As if the towers had thrust aside,
In slightly sinking, the dull tide –
As if their tops had feebly given
A void within the filmy Heaven.
The waves now have a redder glow –

The hours are breathing faint and low —
And when, amid no earthly moans,
Down, down that town shall settle hence,
Hell, rising from a thousand thrones,
Shall do it reverence.

ATLANTIS

There was an island in the sea
That out of immortal chaos reared
Towers of topaz, trees of pearl,
For maidens adored and warriors feared.

Long ago it sunk in the sea;
And now, a thousand fathoms deep,
Sea-worms above it whirl their lamps,
Crabs on the pale mosaic creep.

Voyagers over that haunted sea
Hear from the waters under the keel
A sound that is not wave or foam;
Nor do they only hear, but feel

The timbers quiver, as eerily comes
Up from the dark an elfin singing
Of voices happy as none can be,
And bells an ethereal anthem ringing.

Thereafter, where they go or come,
They will be silent; they have heard
Out of the infinite of the soul
An incommunicable word;

Thereafter, they are as lovers who
Over an infinite brightness lean:
"It is Atlantis!", all their speech;
"To lost Atlantis have we been."

SUNK LYONESSE

In sea-cold Lyonesse,
When the Sabbath eve shafts down
On the roofs, walls, belfries
Of the foundered town,
The Nereids pluck their lyres
Where the green translucency beats,
And with motionless eye at gaze
Make minstrelsy in the streets.

And the ocean water stirs
In salt-worn casemate and porch.
Plies the blunt-snouted fish
With fire in his skull for torch.
And the ringing wires resound;
And the unearthly lovely weep,
In lament of the music they make
In the sullen courts of sleep:
Whose marble flowers bloom for aye:
And – lapped by the moon-guiled tide –
Mock their carver with heart of stone,
Caged in his stone-ribbed side.

ABOVE AND BEYOND

THE BERG
(*A Dream*)

I saw a ship of martial build
(Her standards set, her brave apparel on)
Directed as by madness mere
Against a stolid iceberg steer,
Nor budge it, though the infatuate ship went down.
The impact made huge ice-cubes fall
Sullen, in tons that crashed the deck;
But that one avalanche was all —
No other movement save the foundering wreck.

Along the spurs of ridges pale,
Not any slenderest shaft and frail,
A prism over glass-green gorges lone,
Toppled; nor lace of traceries fine,
Nor pendant drops in grot or mine
Were jarred, when the stunned ship went down.

Nor sole the gulls in cloud that wheeled
Circling one snow-flanked peak afar,
But nearer fowl the floes that skimmed
And crystal beaches, felt no jar.
No thrill transmitted stirred the lock
Of jack-straw needle-ice at base;
Towers undermined by waves — the block

Atilt impending – kept their place.
Seals, dozing sleek on sliddery ledges
Slipt never, when by loftier edges
Through very inertia overthrown,
The impetuous ship in bafflement went down.

Hard Berg (methought), so cold, so vast,
With mortal damps self-overcast;
Exhaling still thy dankish breath –
Adrift dissolving, bound for death;
Though lumpish thou, a lumbering one –
A lumbering lubbard loitering slow,
Impingers rue thee and go down,
Sounding thy precipice below,
Nor stir the slimy slug that sprawls
Along thy dead indifference of walls.

THE TUFT OF KELP

All dripping in tangles green,
    Cast up by a lonely sea,
If purer for that, O Weed,
    Bitterer, too, are ye?

HERMAN MELVILLE

SEAWEED

When descends on the Atlantic
    The gigantic
Storm-wind of the equinox,
Landward in his wrath he scourges
    The toiling surges,
Laden with seaweed from the rocks:

From Bermuda's reefs; from edges
    Of sunken ledges,
In some far-off, bright Azore;
From Bahama, and the dashing,
    Silver-flashing
Surges of San Salvador;

From the tumbling surf, that buries
    The Orkneyan skerries,
Answering the hoarse Hebrides;
And from wrecks of ships, and drifting
    Spars, uplifting
On the desolate, rainy seas; –

Ever drifting, drifting, drifting
    On the shifting
Currents of the restless main;

Till in sheltered coves, and reaches
    Of sandy beaches,
All have found repose again.

So when storms of wild emotion
    Strike the ocean
Of the poet's soul, ere long
From each cave and rocky fastness
    In its vastness,
Floats some fragment of a song:

From the far-off isles enchanted,
    Heaven has planted
With the golden fruit of Truth;
From the flashing surf, whose vision
    Gleams Elysian
In the tropic clime of Youth;

From the strong Will, and the Endeavour
    That for ever
Wrestles with the tides of Fate;
From the wreck of Hopes far-scattered,
    Tempest-shattered,
Floating waste and desolate; –

Ever drifting, drifting, drifting
    On the shifting
Currents of the restless heart;
Till at length in books recorded,
    They, like hoarded
Household words, no more depart.

THE LIGHTHOUSE

The rocky ledge runs far into the sea,
    And on its outer point, some miles away,
The Lighthouse lifts its massive masonry,
    A pillar of fire by night, of cloud by day.

Even at this distance I can see the tides,
    Upheaving, break unheard along its base,
A speechless wrath, that rises and subsides
    In the white lip and tremor of the face.

And as the evening darkens, lo! how bright,
    Through the deep purple of the twilight air,
Beams forth the sudden radiance of its light
    With strange, unearthly splendor in the glare!

Not one alone; from each projecting cape
    And perilous reef along the ocean's verge,
Starts into life a dim, gigantic shape,
    Holding its lantern o'er the restless surge.

Like the great giant Christopher it stands
    Upon the brink of the tempestuous wave,
Wading far out among the rocks and sands,
    The night-o'ertaken mariner to save.

And the great ships sail outward and return,
    Bending and bowing o'er the billowy swells,
And ever joyful, as they see it burn,
    They wave their silent welcomes and farewells.

They come forth from the darkness, and their sails
    Gleam for a moment only in the blaze,
And eager faces, as the light unveils,
    Gaze at the tower, and vanish while they gaze.

The mariner remembers when a child,
    On his first voyage, he saw it fade and sink;
And when, returning from adventures wild,
    He saw it rise again o'er ocean's brink.

Steadfast, serene, immovable, the same
    Year after year, through all the silent night
Burns on forevermore that quenchless flame,
    Shines on that inextinguishable light!

It sees the ocean to its bosom clasp
    The rocks and sea-sand with the kiss of peace;
It sees the wild winds lift it in their grasp,
    And hold it up, and shake it like a fleece.

The startled waves leap over it; the storm
   Smites it with all the scourges of the rain,
And steadily against its solid form
   Press the great shoulders of the hurricane.

The sea-bird wheeling round it, with the din
   Of wings and winds and solitary cries,
Blinded and maddened by the light within,
   Dashes himself against the glare, and dies.

A new Prometheus, chained upon the rock,
   Still grasping in his hand the fire of Jove,
It does not hear the cry, nor heed the shock,
   But hails the mariner with words of love.

"Sail on!" it says, "sail on, ye stately ships!
   And with your floating bridge the ocean span;
Be mine to guard this light from all eclipse,
   Be yours to bring man nearer unto man!"

READING THE WAVES

NEITHER OUT FAR
NOR IN DEEP

The people along the sand
All turn and look one way.
They turn their back on the land.
They look at the sea all day.

As long as it takes to pass
A ship keeps raising its hull;
The wetter ground like glass
Reflects a standing gull.

The land may vary more;
But wherever the truth may be –
The water comes ashore,
And the people look at the sea.

They cannot look out far.
They cannot look in deep.
But when was that ever a bar
To any watch they keep?

ROBERT FROST

A GRAVE

Man looking into the sea,
taking the view from those who have as much right to
    it as you have to it yourself,
it is a human nature to stand in the middle of a thing,
but you cannot stand in the middle of this;
the sea has nothing to give but a well excavated grave.
The firs stand in a procession, each with an emerald
    turkey-foot at the top,
reserved as their contours, saying nothing;
repression, however, is not the most obvious
    characteristic of the sea;
the sea is a collector, quick to return a rapacious look.
There are others besides you who have worn that look –
whose expression is no longer a protest; the fish no
    longer investigate them
for their bones have not lasted:
men lower nets, unconscious of the fact that they are
    desecrating a grave,
and row quickly away – the blades of the oars
moving together like the feet of water-spiders as if
    there were no such thing as death.
The wrinkles progress among themselves in a
    phalanx – beautiful under networks of foam,
and fade breathlessly while the sea rustles in and out of
    the seaweed;

the birds swim through the air at top speed, emitting
    cat-calls as heretofore –
the tortoise-shell scourges about the feet of the cliffs, in
    motion beneath them;
and the ocean, under the pulsation of lighthouses and
    noise of bell-buoys,
advances as usual, looking as if it were not that ocean
    in which dropped things are bound to sink –
in which if they turn and twist, it is neither with
    volition nor consciousness.

MARINE SURFACE,
LOW OVERCAST

Out of churned aureoles
this buttermilk, this
herringbone of albatross,
floss of mercury,
déshabille of spun
aluminum, furred with a velouté
of looking-glass,

a stuff so single
it might almost be lifted,
folded over, crawled underneath
or slid between, as nakedness-
caressing sheets, or donned
and worn, the train-borne
trapping of an unrepeatable
occasion,

this wind-silver
rumpling as of oatfields,
a suede of meadow,
a nub, a nap, a mane of lustre
lithe as the slide
of muscle in its
sheath of skin,

laminae of living tissue,
mysteries of flex,
affinities of texture,
subtleties of touch, of pressure
and release, the suppleness
of long and intimate
association,

new synchronies of fingertip,
of breath, of sequence,
entities that still can rouse,
can stir or solder,
whip to a froth, or force
to march in strictly
hierarchical formation

down galleries of sheen, of flux,
cathedral domes that seem to hover
overturned and shaken like a basin
to the noise of voices,
from a rustle to the jostle
of such rush-hour
conglomerations

no loom, no spinneret, no forge, no factor,
no process whatsoever, patent
applied or not applied for,
no five-year formula, no fabric
for which pure imagining,
except thus prompted,
can invent the equal.

BILLY IN THE DARBIES
From Billy Budd

Good of the Chaplain to enter Lone Bay
And down on his marrow-bones here and pray
For the likes just o' me, Billy Budd. – But, look:
Through the port comes the moon-shine astray!
It tips the guard's cutlass and silvers this nook;
But 'twill die in the dawning of Billy's last day.
A jewel-block they'll make of me tomorrow,
Pendant pearl from the yard-arm-end
Like the ear-drop I gave to Bristol Molly –
O, 'tis me, not the sentence they'll suspend.
Ay, Ay, all is up; and I must up too
Early in the morning, aloft from alow.
On an empty stomach, now, never it would do.
They'll give me a nibble – bit o' biscuit ere I go.
Sure, a messmate will reach me the last parting cup;
But, turning heads away from the hoist and the belay,
Heaven knows who will have the running of me up!
No pipe to those halyards. – But aren't it all sham?
A blur's in my eyes; it is dreaming that I am.
A hatchet to my hawser? All adrift to go?
The drum roll to grog, and Billy never know?
But Donald he has promised to stand by the plank;
So I'll shake a friendly hand ere I sink.
But – no! It is dead then I'll be, come to think. –

I remember Taff the Welshman when he sank.
And his cheek it was like the budding pink.
But me they'll lash in hammock, drop me deep
Fathoms down, fathoms down, how I'll dream
    fast asleep.
I feel it stealing now. Sentry, are you there?
Just ease these darbies at the wrist,
And roll me over fair,
I am sleepy, and the oozy weeds about me twist.

ECHOES

The sea laments
The livelong day,
Fringing its waste of sand;
Cries back the wind from the whispering shore –
No words I understand:
Yet echoes in my heart a voice,
As far, as near, as these –
The wind that weeps,
The solemn surge
Of strange and lonely seas.

"BREAK, BREAK, BREAK"

Break, break, break,
    On thy cold gray stones, O Sea!
And I would that my tongue could utter
    The thoughts that arise in me.

O, well for the fisherman's boy,
    That he shouts with his sister at play!
O, well for the sailor lad,
    That he sings in his boat on the bay!

And the stately ships go on
    To their haven under the hill;
But O for the touch of a vanish'd hand,
    And the sound of a voice that is still!

Break, break, break,
    At the foot of thy crags, O Sea!
But the tender grace of a day that is dead
    Will never come back to me.

SEA-CHANGE

You are no more, but sunken in a sea
Sheer into dream, ten thousand leagues, you fell;
And now you lie green-golden, while a bell
Swings with the tide, my heart; and all is well
Till I look down, and wavering, the spell –
Your loveliness – returns. There in the sea,
Where you lie amber-pale and coral-cool,
You are most loved, most lost, most beautiful.

CROSSING THE BAR

Sunset and evening star,
    And one clear call for me!
And may there be no moaning of the bar,
    When I put out to sea,

But such a tide as moving seems asleep,
    Too full for sound and foam,
When that which drew from out the boundless deep
    Turns again home.

Twilight and evening bell,
    And after that the dark!
And may there be no sadness of farewell,
    When I embark;

For tho' from out our bourne of Time and Place
    The flood may bear me far,
I hope to see my Pilot face to face
    When I have crost the bar.

AT MELVILLE'S TOMB

Often beneath the wave, wide from this ledge
The dice of drowned men's bones he saw bequeath
An embassy. Their numbers as he watched,
Beat on the dusty shore and were obscured.

And wrecks passed without sound of bells,
The calyx of death's bounty giving back
A scattered chapter, livid hieroglyph,
The portent wound in corridors of shells.

Then in the circuit calm of one vast coil,
Its lashings charmed and malice reconciled,
Frosted eyes there were that lifted altars;
And silent answers crept across the stars.

Compass, quadrant and sextant contrive
No farther tides ... High in the azure steeps
Monody shall not wake the mariner.
This fabulous shadow only the sea keeps.

DOVER BEACH

The sea is calm tonight.
The tide is full, the moon lies fair
Upon the straits; – on the French coast the light
Gleams and is gone; the cliffs of England stand,
Glimmering and vast, out in the tranquil bay.
Come to the window, sweet is the night-air!
Only, from the long line of spray
Where the sea meets the moon-blanch'd sand,
Listen! you hear the grating roar
Of pebbles which the waves draw back, and fling,
At their return, up the high strand,
Begin, and cease, and then again begin,
With tremulous cadence slow, and bring
The eternal note of sadness in.

Sophocles long ago
Heard it on the Aegean, and it brought
Into his mind the turbid ebb and flow
Of human misery; we
Find also in the sound a thought,
Hearing it by this distant northern sea.

The sea of faith
Was once, too, at the full, and round earth's shore
Lay like the folds of a bright girdle furl'd.

But now I only hear
Its melancholy, long, withdrawing roar,
Retreating, to the breath
Of the night-winds, down the vast edges drear
And naked shingles of the world.

Ah, love, let us be true
To one another! for the world, which seems
To lie before us like a land of dreams,
So various, so beautiful, so new,
Hath really neither joy, nor love, nor light,
Nor certitude, nor peace, nor help for pain;
And we are here as on a darkling plain
Swept with confus'd alarms of struggle and flight,
Where ignorant armies clash by night.

MATTHEW ARNOLD

PUTTING TO SEA

Who, in the dark, has cast the harbor-chain?
This is no journey to a land we know.
The autumn night receives us, hoarse with rain;
Storm flakes with roaring foam the way we go.

Sodden with summer, stupid with its loves,
The country which we leave, and now this bare
Circle of ocean which the heaven proves
Deep as its height, and barren with despair.

Now this whole silence, through which nothing breaks,
Now this whole sea, which we possess alone,
Flung out from shore with speed a missile takes
When some hard hand, in hatred, flings a stone.

The Way should mark our course within the night,
The streaming System, turned without a sound.
What choice is this – profundity and flight –
Great sea? Our lives through we have trod the ground.

Motion beneath us, fixity above.

"O, but you should rejoice! The course we steer
Points to a beach bright to the rocks with love,
Where, in hot calms, blades clatter on the ear;

And spiny fruits up through the earth are fed
With fire; the palm trees clatter; the wave leaps.
Fleeing a shore where heart-loathed love lies dead
We point lands where love fountains from its deeps.

Through every season the coarse fruits are set
In earth not fed by streams." Soft into time
Once broke the flower: pear and violet,
The cinquefoil. The tall elm tree and the lime

Once held out fruitless boughs, and fluid green
Once rained about us, pulse of earth indeed.
There, out of metal, and to light obscene,
The flamy blooms burn backwards to their seed.

With so much hated still so close behind
The sterile shores before us must be faced;
Again, against the body and the mind,
The hate that bruises, though the heart is braced.

Bend to the chart, in the extinguished night
Mariners! Make way slowly; stay from sleep;
That we may have short respite from such light.

And learn, with joy, the gulf, the vast, the deep.

LOUISE BOGAN

"I STARTED EARLY"

I started early, took my dog,
And visited the sea –
The Mermaids in the basement
Came out to look at me,

And Frigates in the upper floor
Extended hempen hands –
Presuming me to be a mouse
Aground, upon the sands.

But no man moved me till the Tide
Went past my simple shoe,
And past my apron and my belt
And past my bodice too –

And made as he would eat me up
As wholly as a dew
Upon a dandelion's sleeve –
And then I started too.

And he – he followed close behind –
I felt his silver heel
Upon my ankle – then my shoes
Would overflow with pearl.

Until we met the solid town,
No man he seemed to know –
And bowing with a mighty look
At me, the Sea withdrew.

NOT WAVING BUT DROWNING

Nobody heard him, the dead man,
But still he lay moaning:
I was much further out than you thought
And not waving but drowning.

Poor chap, he always loved larking
And now he's dead
It must have been too cold for him his heart gave way,
They said.

Oh, no no no, it was too cold always
(Still the dead one lay moaning)
I was much too far out all my life
And not waving but drowning.

THE IDEA OF ORDER AT KEY WEST

She sang beyond the genius of the sea.
The water never formed to mind or voice,
Like a body wholly body, fluttering
Its empty sleeves; and yet its mimic motion
Made constant cry, caused constantly a cry,
That was not ours although we understood,
Inhuman, of the veritable ocean.

The sea was not a mask. No more was she.
The song and water were not medleyed sound
Even if what she sang was what she heard,
Since what she sang was uttered word by word.
It may be that in all her phrases stirred
The grinding water and the gasping wind;
But it was she and not the sea we heard.

For she was the maker of the song she sang.
The ever-hooded, tragic-gestured sea
Was merely a place by which she walked to sing.
Whose spirit is this? we said, because we knew
It was the spirit that we sought and knew
That we should ask this often as she sang.

If it was only the dark voice of the sea
That rose, or even colored by many waves;

If it was only the outer voice of sky
And cloud, of the sunken coral water-walled,
However clear, it would have been deep air,
The heaving speech of air, a summer sound
Repeated in a summer without end
And sound alone. But it was more than that,
More even than her voice, and ours, among
The meaningless plungings of water and the wind,
Theatrical distances, bronze shadows heaped
On high horizons, mountainous atmospheres
Of sky and sea.

               It was her voice that made
The sky acutest at its vanishing.
She measured to the hour its solitude.
She was the single artificer of the world
In which she sang. And when she sang, the sea,
Whatever self it had, became the self
That was her song, for she was the maker. Then we,
As we beheld her striding there alone,
Knew that there never was a world for her
Except the one she sang and, singing, made.

Ramon Fernandez, tell me, if you know,
Why, when the singing ended and we turned
Toward the town, tell why the glassy lights,
The lights in the fishing boats at anchor there,
As the night descended, tilting in the air,

Mastered the night and portioned out the sea,
Fixing emblazoned zones and fiery poles,
Arranging, deepening, enchanting night.

Oh! Blessed rage for order, pale Ramon,
The maker's rage to order words of the sea,
Words of the fragrant portals, dimly-starred,
And of ourselves and of our origins,
In ghostlier demarcations, keener sounds.

WALLACE STEVENS   233

MARINA

Quis hic locus, quae regio, quae mundi plaga?

What seas what shores what grey rocks and
    what islands
What water lapping the bow
And scent of pine and the woodthrush singing
    through the fog
What images return
O my daughter.

   Those who sharpen the tooth of the dog,
     meaning
Death
Those who glitter with the glory of the humming-bird,
     meaning
Death
Those who sit in the sty of contentment,
     meaning
Death
Those who suffer the ecstasy of the animals,
     meaning
Death

   Are become unsubstantial, reduced by a wind,
A breath of pine, and the woodsong fog
By this grace dissolved in place

What is this face, less clear and clearer
The pulse in the arm, less strong and stronger –
Given or lent? more distant than stars and nearer
    than the eye

   Whispers and small laughter between leaves
     and hurrying feet
Under sleep, where all the waters meet.

   Bowsprit cracked with ice and paint cracked
     with heat.
I made this, I have forgotten
And remember.
The rigging weak and the canvas rotten
Between one June and another September.
Made this unknowing, half conscious, unknown,
    my own.
The garboard strake leaks, the seams need caulking.

This form, this face, this life
Living to live in a world of time beyond me; let me
Resign my life for this life, my speech for that unspoken,
The awakened, lips parted, the hope, the new ships.

   What seas what shores what granite islands
     towards my timbers
And woodthrush calling through the fog
My daughter.

AS I EBB'D WITH THE OCEAN OF LIFE

1

As I ebb'd with the ocean of life,
As I wended the shores I know,
As I walk'd where the ripples continually wash you
    Paumanok,
Where they rustle up hoarse and sibilant,
Where the fierce old mother endlessly cries
    for her castaways,
I musing late in the autumn day, gazing off southward,
Held by this electric self out of the pride of which
    I utter poems,
Was seiz'd by the spirit that trails in the lines underfoot,
The rim, the sediment that stands for all the water and
    all the land of the globe.

Fascinated, my eyes reverting from the south, dropt,
    to follow those slender windrows,
Chaff, straw, splinters of wood, weeds, and
    the sea-gluten,
Scum, scales from shining rocks, leaves of
    salt-lettuce, left by the tide,
Miles walking, the sound of breaking waves
    the other side of me,
Paumanok there and then as I thought the old thought
    of likenesses,

These you presented to me you fish-shaped island,
As I wended the shores I know,
As I walk'd with that electric self seeking types.

2

As I wend to the shores I know not,
As I list to the dirge, the voices of men and women
      wreck'd,
As I inhale the impalpable breezes that set in upon me,
As the ocean so mysterious rolls toward me closer
      and closer,
I too but signify at the utmost a little wash'd-up drift,
A few sands and dead leaves to gather,
Gather, and merge myself as part of the sands and drift.

O baffled, balk'd, bent to the very earth,
Oppress'd with myself that I have dared to open
      my mouth,
Aware now that amid all that blab whose echoes recoil
      upon me I have not once had the least idea who
      or what I am,
But that before all my arrogant poems the real Me
      stands yet untouch'd, untold, altogether unreach'd,
Withdrawn far, mocking me with mock-congratulatory
      signs and bows,

With peals of distant ironical laughter at every word
  I have written,
Pointing in silence to these songs, and then to
  the sand beneath.

I perceive I have not really understood any thing,
  not a single object, and that no man ever can,
Nature here in sight of the sea taking advantage of me
  to dart upon me and sting me,
Because I have dared to open my mouth to sing at all.

3

You oceans both, I close with you,
We murmur alike reproachfully rolling sands and drift,
  knowing not why,
These little shreds indeed standing for you and me
  and all.

You friable shore with trails of debris,
You fish-shaped island, I take what is underfoot,
What is yours is mine my father.

I too Paumanok,
I too have bubbled up, floated the measureless float,
  and been wash'd on your shores,
I too am but a trail of drift and debris,
I too leave little wrecks upon you, you fish-shaped island.

I throw myself upon your breast my father,
I cling to you so that you cannot unloose me,
I hold you so firm till you answer me something.

Kiss me my father,
Touch me with your lips as I touch those I love,
Breathe to me while I hold you close the secret of
       the murmuring I envy.

4

Ebb, ocean of life, (the flow will return,)
Cease not your moaning you fierce old mother,
Endlessly cry for your castaways, but fear not, deny
       not me,
Rustle not up so hoarse and angry against my feet
       as I touch you or gather from you.

I mean tenderly by you and all,
I gather for myself and for this phantom looking down
       where we lead, and following me and mine.

Me and mine, loose windrows, little corpses,
Froth, snowy white, and bubbles,
(See, from my dead lips the ooze exuding at last,
See, the prismatic colors glistening and rolling,)
Tufts of straw, sands, fragments,
Buoy'd hither from many moods, one contradicting
       another,

From the storm, the long calm, the darkness, the swell,
Musing, pondering, a breath, a briny tear, a dab
    of liquid or soil,
Up just as much out of fathomless workings fermented
    and thrown,
A limp blossom or two, torn, just as much over waves
    floating, drifted at random,
Just as much for us that sobbing dirge of Nature,
Just as much whence we come that blare of the
    cloud-trumpets,
We, capricious, brought hither we know not whence,
    spread out before you,
You up there walking or sitting,
Whoever you are, we too lie in drifts at your feet.

ACKNOWLEDGMENTS

Thanks are due to the following copyright holders for their permission to reprint:

INDEX OF AUTHORS